The Pelican Shakespeare
General Editors

STEPHEN ORGEL
A. R. BRAUNMULLER

Coriolanus

Ellen Terry as Volumnia, 1901

William Shakespeare

Coriolanus

EDITED BY JONATHAN CREWE

PENGUIN BOOKS

PENGUIN BOOKS
Published by the Penguin Group
Penguin Group (USA) Inc., 375 Hudson Street, New York, New York 10014, U.S.A.
Penguin Group (Canada), 90 Eglinton Avenue East, Suite 700, Toronto, Ontario,
Canada M4P 2Y3 (a division of Pearson Penguin Canada Inc.)
Penguin Books Ltd, 80 Strand, London WC2R 0RL, England
Penguin Ireland, 25 St Stephen's Green, Dublin 2, Ireland (a division of Penguin Books Ltd)
Penguin Group (Australia), 250 Camberwell Road, Camberwell,
Victoria 3124, Australia (a division of Pearson Australia Group Pty Ltd)
Penguin Books India Pvt Ltd, 11 Community Centre, Panchsheel Park,
New Delhi – 110 017, India
Penguin Group (NZ), 67 Apollo Drive, Rosedale, North Shore 0632, New Zealand
(a division of Pearson New Zealand Ltd)
Penguin Books (South Africa) (Pty) Ltd, 24 Sturdee Avenue, Rosebank,
Johannesburg 2196, South Africa

Penguin Books Ltd, Registered Offices: 80 Strand, London WC2R 0RL, England

The Tragedy of Coriolanus edited by Harry Levin published in
the United States of America in Penguin Books 1956
Revised edition published 1973
This new edition edited by Jonathan Crewe published 1999

13   15   17   19   20   18   16   14   12

Copyright © Penguin Books Inc., 1956, 1973
Copyright © Penguin Putnam Inc., 1999
All rights reserved

ISBN 978-0-14-071473-9

Printed in the United States of America
Set in Garamond
Designed by Virginia Norey

Contents

Publisher's Note

IT IS ALMOST half a century since the first volumes of the Pelican Shakespeare appeared under the general editorship of Alfred Harbage. The fact that a new edition, rather than simply a revision, has been undertaken reflects the profound changes textual and critical studies of Shakespeare have undergone in the past twenty years. For the new Pelican series, the texts of the plays and poems have been thoroughly revised in accordance with recent scholarship, and in some cases have been entirely reedited. New introductions and notes have been provided in all the volumes. But the new Shakespeare is also designed as a successor to the original series; the previous editions have been taken into account, and the advice of the previous editors has been solicited where it was feasible to do so.

Certain textual features of the new Pelican Shakespeare should be particularly noted. All lines are numbered that contain a word, phrase, or allusion explained in the glossarial notes. In addition, for convenience, every tenth line is also numbered, in italics when no annotation is indicated. The intrusive and often inaccurate place headings inserted by early editors are omitted (as is becoming standard practice), but for the convenience of those who miss them, an indication of locale now appears as the first item in the annotation of each scene.

In the interest of both elegance and utility, each speech prefix is set in a separate line when the speaker's lines are in verse, except when those words form the second half of a verse line. Thus the verse form of the speech is kept visually intact. What is printed as verse and what is printed as prose has, in general, the authority of the original texts. Departures from the original texts in this regard have only the authority of editorial tradition and the judgment of the Pelican editors; and, in a few instances, are admittedly arbitrary.

The Theatrical World

ECONOMIC REALITIES determined the theatrical world in which Shakespeare's plays were written, performed, and received. For centuries in England, the primary theatrical tradition was nonprofessional. Craft guilds (or "mysteries") provided religious drama – mystery plays – as part of the celebration of religious and civic festivals, and schools and universities staged classical and neoclassical drama in both Latin and English as part of their curricula. In these forms, drama was established and socially acceptable. Professional theater, in contrast, existed on the margins of society. The acting companies were itinerant; playhouses could be any available space – the great halls of the aristocracy, town squares, civic halls, inn yards, fair booths, or open fields – and income was sporadic, dependent on the passing of the hat or on the bounty of local patrons. The actors, moreover, were considered little better than vagabonds, constantly in danger of arrest or expulsion.

In the late 1560s and 1570s, however, English professional theater began to gain respectability. Wealthy aristocrats fond of drama – the Lord Admiral, for example, or the Lord Chamberlain – took acting companies under their protection so that the players technically became members of their households and were no longer subject to arrest as homeless or masterless men. Permanent theaters were first built at this time as well, allowing the companies to control and charge for entry to their performances.

Shakespeare's livelihood, and the stunning artistic explosion in which he participated, depended on pragmatic and architectural effort. Professional theater requires ways to restrict access to its offerings; if it does not, and admission fees cannot be charged, the actors do not get paid, the costumes go to a pawnbroker, and there is no such thing as a professional, ongoing theatrical tradition. The answer to that economic need arrived in the late 1560s and 1570s with the creation of the so-called public or amphitheater playhouse. Recent discoveries indicate that the precursor of the Globe playhouse in London (where Shakespeare's mature plays were presented) and the Rose theater (which presented Christopher Marlowe's plays and some of Shakespeare's earliest ones) was the Red Lion theater of 1567. Archaeological studies of the foundations of the Rose and Globe theaters have revealed that the open-air theater of the 1590s and later was probably a polygonal building with fourteen to twenty or twenty-four sides, multistoried, from 75 to 100 feet in diameter, with a raised, partly covered "thrust" stage that projected into a group of standing patrons, or "groundlings," and a covered gallery, seating up to 2,500 or more (very crowded) spectators.

These theaters might have been about half full on any given day, though the audiences were larger on holidays or when a play was advertised, as old and new were, through printed playbills posted around London. The metropolitan area's late-Tudor, early-Stuart population (circa 1590-1620) has been estimated at about 150,000 to 250,000. It has been supposed that in the mid-1590s there were about 15,000 spectators per week at the public theaters; thus, as many as 10 percent of the local population went to the theater regularly. Consequently, the theaters' repertories – the plays available for this experienced and frequent audience – had to change often: in the month between September 15 and October 15, 1595, for instance, the Lord Admiral's Men performed twenty-eight times in eighteen different plays.

Since natural light illuminated the amphitheaters' stages, performances began between noon and two o'clock and ran without a break for two or three hours. They often concluded with a jig, a fencing display, or some other nondramatic exhibition. Weather conditions determined the season for the amphitheaters: plays were performed every day (including Sundays, sometimes, to clerical dismay) except during Lent – the forty days before Easter – or periods of plague, or sometimes during the summer months when law courts were not in session and the most affluent members of the audience were not in London.

To a modern theatergoer, an amphitheater stage like that of the Rose or Globe would appear an unfamiliar mixture of plainness and elaborate decoration. Much of the structure was carved or painted, sometimes to imitate marble; elsewhere, as under the canopy projecting over the stage, to represent the stars and the zodiac. Appropriate painted canvas pictures (of Jerusalem, for example, if the play was set in that city) were apparently hung on the wall behind the acting area, and tragedies were accompanied by black hangings, presumably something like crepe festoons or bunting. Although these theaters did not employ what we would call scenery, early modern spectators saw numerous large props, such as the "bar" at which a prisoner stood during a trial, the "mossy bank" where lovers reclined, an arbor for amorous conversation, a chariot, gallows, tables, trees, beds, thrones, writing desks, and so forth. Audiences might learn a scene's location from a sign (reading "Athens," for example) carried across the stage (as in Bertolt Brecht's twentieth-century productions). Equally captivating (and equally irritating to the theater's enemies) were the rich costumes and personal props the actors used: the most valuable items in the surviving theatrical inventories are the swords, gowns, robes, crowns, and other items worn or carried by the performers.

Magic appealed to Shakespeare's audiences as much as it does to us today, and the theater exploited many deceptive and spectacular devices. A winch in the loft above the stage, called "the heavens," could lower and raise actors playing gods, goddesses, and other supernatural figures to and from the main acting area, just as one or more trapdoors permitted entrances and exits to and from the area, called "hell," beneath the stage. Actors wore elementary makeup such as wigs, false beards, and face paint, and they employed pig's bladders filled with animal blood to make wounds seem more real. They had rudimentary but effective ways of pretending to behead or hang a person. Supernumeraries (stagehands or actors not needed in a particular scene) could make thunder sounds (by shaking a metal sheet or rolling an iron ball down a chute) and show lightning (by blowing inflammable resin through tubes into a flame). Elaborate fireworks enhanced the effects of dragons flying through the air or imitated such celestial phenomena as comets, shooting stars, and multiple suns. Horses' hoofbeats, bells (located perhaps in the tower above the stage), trumpets and drums, clocks, cannon shots and gunshots, and the like were common sound effects. And the music of viols, cornets, oboes, and recorders was a regular feature of theatrical performances.

For two relatively brief spans, from the late 1570s to 1590 and from 1599 to 1614, the amphitheaters competed with the so-called private, or indoor, theaters, which originated as, or later represented themselves as, educational institutions training boys as singers for church services and court performances. These indoor theaters had two features that were distinct from the amphitheaters': their personnel and their playing spaces. The amphitheaters' adult companies included both adult men, who played the male roles, and boys, who played the female roles; the private, or indoor, theater companies, on the other hand, were entirely composed of boys aged about 8 to 16, who were, or could pretend to be, candidates for singers in a church or a royal boys' choir. (Until 1660, professional theatrical companies included no women.) The playing space would appear much more familiar to modern audiences than the long-vanished amphitheaters; the later indoor theaters were, in fact, the ancestors of the typical modern theater. They were enclosed spaces, usually rectangular, with the stage filling one end of the rectangle and the audience arrayed in seats or benches across (and sometimes lining) the building's longer axis. These spaces staged plays less frequently than the public theaters (perhaps only once a week) and held far fewer spectators than the amphitheaters: about 200 to 600, as opposed to 2,500 or more. Fewer patrons mean a smaller gross income, unless each pays more. Not surprisingly, then, private theaters charged higher prices than the amphitheaters, probably sixpence, as opposed to a penny for the cheapest entry.

Protected from the weather, the indoor theaters presented plays later in the day than the amphitheaters, and used artificial illumination – candles in sconces or candelabra. But candles melt, and need replacing, snuffing, and trimming, and these practical requirements may have been part of the reason the indoor theaters introduced breaks in the performance, the intermission so dear to the heart of theatergoers and to the pocketbooks of theater concessionaires ever since. Whether motivated by the need to tend to the candles or by the entrepreneurs' wishing to sell oranges and liquor, or both, the indoor theaters eventually established the modern convention of the non-continuous performance. In the early modern "private" theater, musical performances apparently filled the intermissions, which in Stuart theater jargon seem to have been called "acts."

At the end of the first decade of the seventeenth century, the distinction between public amphitheaters and private indoor companies ceased. For various cultural, political, and economic reasons, individual companies gained control of both the public, open-air theaters and the indoor ones, and companies mixing adult men and boys took over the formerly "private" theaters. Despite the death of the boys' companies and of their highly innovative theaters (for which such luminous playwrights as Ben Jonson, George Chapman, and John Marston wrote), their playing spaces and conventions had an immense impact on subsequent plays: not merely for the intervals (which stressed the artistic and architectonic importance of "acts"), but also because they introduced political and social satire as a popular dramatic ingredient, even in tragedy, and a wider range of actorly effects, encouraged by their more intimate playing spaces.

Even the briefest sketch of the Shakespearean theatrical world would be incomplete without some comment on the social and cultural dimensions of theaters and playing in the period. In an intensely hierarchical and status-conscious society, professional actors and their ventures had hardly any respectability; as we have indicated, to protect themselves against laws designed to curb vagabondage and the increase of masterless men, actors resorted to the near-fiction that they were the servants of noble masters, and wore their distinctive livery. Hence the company for which Shakespeare wrote in the 1590s called itself the Lord Chamberlain's Men and pretended that the public, money-getting performances were in fact rehearsals for private performances before that high court official. From 1598, the Privy Council had licensed theatrical companies, and after 1603, with the accession of King James I, the companies gained explicit royal protection, just as the Queen's Men had for a time under Queen Elizabeth. The Chamberlain's Men became the King's Men, and the other companies were patronized by the other members of the royal family.

These designations were legal fictions that half-concealed an important economic and social development, the evolution away from the theater's organization on the model of the guild, a self-regulating confraternity of individual artisans, into a proto-capitalist organization. Shakespeare's company became a joint-stock company, where persons who supplied capital and, in some cases, such as Shakespeare's, capital and talent, employed themselves and others in earning a return on that capital. This development meant that actors and theater companies were outside both the traditional guild structures, which required some form of civic or royal charter, and the feudal household organization of master-and-servant. This anomalous, maverick social and economic condition made theater companies practically unruly and potentially even dangerous; consequently, numerous official bodies – including the London metropolitan and ecclesiastical authorities as well as, occasionally, the royal court itself – tried, without much success, to control and even to disband them.

Public officials had good reason to want to close the theaters: they were attractive nuisances – they drew often riotous crowds, they were always noisy, and they could be politically offensive and socially insubordinate. Until the Civil War, however, anti-theatrical forces failed to shut down professional theater, for many reasons – limited surveillance and few police powers, tensions or outright hostilities among the agencies that sought to check or channel theatrical activity, and lack of clear policies for control. Another reason must have been the theaters' undeniable popularity. Curtailing any activity enjoyed by such a substantial percentage of the population was difficult, as various Roman emperors attempting to limit circuses had learned, and the Tudor-Stuart audience was not merely large, it was socially diverse and included women. The prevalence of public entertainment in this period has been underestimated. In fact, fairs, holidays, games, sporting events, the equivalent of modern parades, freak shows, and street exhibitions all abounded, but the theater was the most widely and frequently available entertainment to which people of every class had access. That fact helps account both for its quantity and for the fear and anger it aroused.

WILLIAM SHAKESPEARE OF STRATFORD-UPON-AVON, GENTLEMAN

Many people have said that we know very little about William Shakespeare's life – pinheads and postcards are often mentioned as appropriately tiny surfaces on which to record the available information. More imaginatively and perhaps more correctly, Ralph Waldo Emerson wrote, "Shakespeare is the only biographer of Shakespeare. . . . So far from Shakespeare's being the least known, he is the one person in all modern history fully known to us."

In fact, we know more about Shakespeare's life than we do about almost any other English writer's of his era. His last will and testament (dated March 25, 1616) survives, as do numerous legal contracts and court documents involving Shakespeare as principal or witness, and parish records in Stratford and London. Shakespeare appears quite often in official records of King James's royal court, and of course Shakespeare's name appears on numerous title pages and in the written and recorded words of his literary contemporaries Robert Greene, Henry Chettle, Francis Meres, John Davies of Hereford, Ben Jonson, and many others. Indeed, if we make due allowance for the bloating of modern, run-of-the-mill bureaucratic records, more information has survived over the past four hundred years about William Shakespeare of Stratford-upon-Avon, Warwickshire, than is likely to survive in the next four hundred years about any reader of these words.

What we do not have are entire categories of information – Shakespeare's private letters or diaries, drafts and revisions of poems and plays, critical prefaces or essays, commendatory verse for other writers' works, or instructions guiding his fellow actors in their performances, for instance – that we imagine would help us understand and appreciate his surviving writings. For all we know, many such data never existed as written records. Many literary and theatrical critics, not knowing what might once have existed, more or less cheerfully accept the situation; some even make a theoretical virtue of it by claiming that such data are irrelevant to understanding and interpreting the plays and poems.

So, what do we know about William Shakespeare, the man responsible for thirty-seven or perhaps more plays, more than 150 sonnets, two lengthy narrative poems, and some shorter poems?

While many families by the name of Shakespeare (or some variant spelling) can be identified in the English Midlands as far back as the twelfth century, it seems likely that the dramatist's grandfather, Richard, moved to Snitterfield, a town not far from Stratford-upon-Avon, sometime before 1529. In Snitterfield, Richard Shakespeare leased farmland from the very wealthy Robert Arden. By 1552, Richard's son John had moved to a large house on Henley Street in Stratford-upon-Avon, the house that stands today as "The Birthplace." In Stratford, John Shakespeare traded as a glover, dealt in wool, and lent money at interest; he also served in a variety of civic posts, including "High Bailiff," the municipality's equivalent of mayor. In 1557, he married Robert Arden's youngest daughter, Mary. Mary and John had four sons – William was the oldest – and four daughters, of whom only Joan outlived her most celebrated sibling. William was baptized (an event entered in the Stratford parish church records) on April 26, 1564, and it has become customary, without any good factual support, to suppose he was born on April 23, which happens to be the feast day of Saint George, patron saint of England, and is also the date on which he died, in 1616. Shakespeare married Anne Hathaway in 1582, when he was eighteen and she was twenty-six; their first child was born five months later. It has been generally assumed that the marriage was enforced and subsequently unhappy, but these are only assumptions; it has been estimated, for instance, that up to one third of Elizabethan brides were pregnant when they married. Anne and William Shakespeare had three children: Susanna, who married a prominent local physician, John Hall; and the twins Hamnet, who died young in 1596, and Judith, who married Thomas Quiney – apparently a rather shady individual. The name Hamnet was unusual but not unique: he and his twin sister were named for their godparents, Shakespeare's neighbors Hamnet and Judith Sadler. Shakespeare's father died in 1601 (the year of *Hamlet*), and Mary Arden Shakespeare died in 1608

(the year of *Coriolanus*). William Shakespeare's last surviving direct descendant was his granddaughter Elizabeth
Hall, who died in 1670.

Between the birth of the twins in 1585 and a clear reference to Shakespeare as a practicing London dramatist in
Robert Greene's sensationalizing, satiric pamphlet, *Greene's
Groatsworth of Wit* (1592), there is no record of where
William Shakespeare was or what he was doing. These
seven so-called lost years have been imaginatively filled by
scholars and other students of Shakespeare: some think
he traveled to Italy, or fought in the Low Countries, or
studied law or medicine, or worked as an apprentice
actor/writer, and so on to even more fanciful possibilities.
Whatever the biographical facts for those "lost" years,
Greene's nasty remarks in 1592 testify to professional envy
and to the fact that Shakespeare already had a successful career in London. Speaking to his fellow playwrights, Greene
warns both generally and specifically:

> . . . trust them [actors] not: for there is an upstart
> crow, beautified with our feathers, that with his
> tiger's heart wrapped in a player's hide supposes he is
> as well able to bombast out a blank verse as the best
> of you; and being an absolute Johannes Factotum, is
> in his own conceit the only Shake-scene in a country.

The passage mimics a line from *3 Henry VI* (hence the play
must have been performed before Greene wrote) and
seems to say that "Shake-scene" is both actor and playwright, a jack-of-all-trades. That same year, Henry Chettle
protested Greene's remarks in *Kind-Heart's Dream,* and
each of the next two years saw the publication of poems –
Venus and Adonis and *The Rape of Lucrece,* respectively –
publicly ascribed to (and dedicated by) Shakespeare. Early
in 1595 he was named one of the senior members of a
prominent acting company, the Lord Chamberlain's Men,
when they received payment for court performances during the 1594 Christmas season.

Clearly, Shakespeare had achieved both success and reputation in London. In 1596, upon Shakespeare's application, the College of Arms granted his father the now-familiar coat of arms he had taken the first steps to obtain almost twenty years before, and in 1598, John's son – now permitted to call himself "gentleman" – took a 10 percent share in the new Globe playhouse. In 1597, he bought a substantial bourgeois house, called New Place, in Stratford – the garden remains, but Shakespeare's house, several times rebuilt, was torn down in 1759 – and over the next few years Shakespeare spent large sums buying land and making other investments in the town and its environs. Though he worked in London, his family remained in Stratford, and he seems always to have considered Stratford the home he would eventually return to. Something approaching a disinterested appreciation of Shakespeare's popular and professional status appears in Francis Meres's *Palladis Tamia* (1598), a not especially imaginative and perhaps therefore persuasive record of literary reputations. Reviewing contemporary English writers, Meres lists the titles of many of Shakespeare's plays, including one not now known, *Love's Labor's Won,* and praises his "mellifluous & hony-tongued" "sugred Sonnets," which were then circulating in manuscript (they were first collected in 1609). Meres describes Shakespeare as "one of the best" English playwrights of both comedy and tragedy. In *Remains . . . Concerning Britain* (1605), William Camden – a more authoritative source than the imitative Meres – calls Shakespeare one of the "most pregnant witts of these our times" and joins him with such writers as Chapman, Daniel, Jonson, Marston, and Spenser. During the first decades of the seventeenth century, publishers began to attribute numerous play quartos, including some non-Shakespearean ones, to Shakespeare, either by name or initials, and we may assume that they deemed Shakespeare's name and supposed authorship, true or false, commercially attractive.

For the next ten years or so, various records show

Shakespeare's dual career as playwright and man of the theater in London, and as an important local figure in Stratford. In 1608-9 his acting company – designated the "King's Men" soon after King James had succeeded Queen Elizabeth in 1603 – rented, refurbished, and opened a small interior playing space, the Blackfriars theater, in London, and Shakespeare was once again listed as a substantial sharer in the group of proprietors of the playhouse. By May 11, 1612, however, he describes himself as a Stratford resident in a London lawsuit – an indication that he had withdrawn from day-to-day professional activity and returned to the town where he had always had his main financial interests. When Shakespeare bought a substantial residential building in London, the Blackfriars Gatehouse, close to the theater of the same name, on March 10, 1613, he is recorded as William Shakespeare "of Stratford upon Avon in the county of Warwick, gentleman," and he named several London residents as the building's trustees. Still, he continued to participate in theatrical activity: when the new Earl of Rutland needed an allegorical design to bear as a shield, or *impresa,* at the celebration of King James's Accession Day, March 24, 1613, the earl's accountant recorded a payment of 44 shillings to Shakespeare for the device with its motto.

For the last few years of his life, Shakespeare evidently concentrated his activities in the town of his birth. Most of the final records concern business transactions in Stratford, ending with the notation of his death on April 23, 1616, and burial in Holy Trinity Church, Stratford-upon-Avon.

THE QUESTION OF AUTHORSHIP

The history of ascribing Shakespeare's plays (the poems do not come up so often) to someone else began, as it continues, peculiarly. The earliest published claim that someone else wrote Shakespeare's plays appeared in an 1856 article by Delia Bacon in the American journal *Putnam's Monthly* – although an Englishman, Thomas Wilmot, had shared his doubts in private (even secretive) conversations with friends near the end of the eighteenth century. Bacon's was a sad personal history that ended in madness and poverty, but the year after her article, she published, with great difficulty and the bemused assistance of Nathaniel Hawthorne (then United States Consul in Liverpool, England), her *Philosophy of the Plays of Shakspere Unfolded.* This huge, ornately written, confusing farrago is almost unreadable; sometimes its intents, to say nothing of its arguments, disappear entirely beneath near-raving, ecstatic writing. Tumbled in with much supposed "philosophy" appear the claims that Francis Bacon (from whom Delia Bacon eventually claimed descent), Walter Ralegh, and several other contemporaries of Shakespeare's had written the plays. The book had little impact except as a ridiculed curiosity.

Once proposed, however, the issue gained momentum among people whose conviction was the greater in proportion to their ignorance of sixteenth- and seventeenth-century English literature, history, and society. Another American amateur, Catherine P. Ashmead Windle, made the next influential contribution to the cause when she published *Report to the British Museum* (1882), wherein she promised to open "the Cipher of Francis Bacon," though what she mostly offers, in the words of S. Schoenbaum, is "demented allegorizing." An entire new cottage industry grew from Windle's suggestion that the texts contain hidden, cryptographically discoverable ciphers – "clues" – to their authorship; and today there are not only books devoted to the putative ciphers, but also pamphlets, journals, and newsletters.

Although Baconians have led the pack of those seeking a substitute Shakespeare, in *"Shakespeare" Identified* (1920), J. Thomas Looney became the first published

"Oxfordian" when he proposed Edward de Vere, seventeenth earl of Oxford, as the secret author of Shakespeare's plays. Also for Oxford and his "authorship" there are today dedicated societies, articles, journals, and books. Less popular candidates – Queen Elizabeth and Christopher Marlowe among them – have had adherents, but the movement seems to have divided into two main contending factions, Baconian and Oxfordian. (For further details on all the candidates for "Shakespeare," see S. Schoenbaum, *Shakespeare's Lives*, 2nd ed., 1991.)

The Baconians, the Oxfordians, and supporters of other candidates have one trait in common – they are snobs. Every pro-Bacon or pro-Oxford tract sooner or later claims that the historical William Shakespeare of Stratford-upon-Avon could not have written the plays because he could not have had the training, the university education, the experience, and indeed the imagination or background their author supposedly possessed. Only a learned genius like Bacon or an aristocrat like Oxford could have written such fine plays. (As it happens, lucky male children of the middle class had access to better education than most aristocrats in Elizabethan England – and Oxford was not particularly well educated.) Shakespeare received in the Stratford grammar school a formal education that would daunt many college graduates today; and popular rival playwrights such as the very learned Ben Jonson and George Chapman, both of whom also lacked university training, achieved great artistic success, without being taken as Bacon or Oxford.

Besides snobbery, one other quality characterizes the authorship controversy: lack of evidence. A great deal of testimony from Shakespeare's time shows that Shakespeare wrote Shakespeare's plays and that his contemporaries recognized them as distinctive and distinctly superior. (Some of that contemporary evidence is collected in E. K. Chambers, *William Shakespeare: A Study of Facts and Problems*, 2 vols., 1930.) Since that testimony comes from Shakespeare's enemies and theatrical competitors as well as from his co-workers and from the Elizabethan equivalent of literary journalists, it seems unlikely that, if any one of these sources had known he was a fraud, they would have failed to record that fact.

Books About Shakespeare's Theater

Useful scholarly studies of theatrical life in Shakespeare's day include: G. E. Bentley, *The Jacobean and Caroline Stage*, 7 vols. (1941-68), and the same author's *The Professions of Dramatist and Player in Shakespeare's Time, 1590-1642* (1986); E. K. Chambers, *The Elizabethan Stage*, 4 vols. (1923); R. A. Foakes, *Illustrations of the English Stage, 1580-1642* (1985); Andrew Gurr, *The Shakespearean Stage*, 3rd ed. (1992), and the same author's *Play-going in Shakespeare's London*, 2nd ed. (1996); Edwin Nungezer, *A Dictionary of Actors* (1929); Carol Chillington Rutter, ed., *Documents of the Rose Playhouse* (1984).

Books About Shakespeare's Life

The following books provide scholarly, documented accounts of Shakespeare's life: G. E. Bentley, *Shakespeare: A Biographical Handbook* (1961); E. K. Chambers, *William Shakespeare: A Study of Facts and Problems*, 2 vols. (1930); S. Schoenbaum, *William Shakespeare: A Compact Documentary Life* (1977); and *Shakespeare's Lives*, 2nd ed. (1991), by the same author. Many scholarly editions of Shakespeare's complete works print brief compilations of essential dates and events. References to Shakespeare's works up to 1700 are collected in C. M. Ingleby et al., *The Shakespeare Allusion-Book*, rev. ed., 2 vols. (1932).

The Texts of Shakespeare

As far as we know, only one manuscript conceivably in Shakespeare's own hand may (and even this is much disputed) exist: a few pages of a play called *Sir Thomas More*, which apparently was never performed. What we do have, as later readers, performers, scholars, students, are printed texts. The earliest of these survive in two forms: quartos and folios. Quartos (from the Latin for "four") are small books, printed on sheets of paper that were then folded twice, to make four leaves or eight pages. When these were bound together, the result was a squarish, eminently portable volume that sold for the relatively small sum of sixpence (translating in modern terms to about $5.00). In folios, on the other hand, the sheets are folded only once, in half, producing large, impressive volumes taller than they are wide. This was the format for important works of philosophy, science, theology, and literature (the major precedent for a folio Shakespeare was Ben Jonson's *Works*, 1616). The decision to print the works of a popular playwright in folio is an indication of how far up on the social scale the theatrical profession had come during Shakespeare's lifetime. The Shakespeare folio was an expensive book, selling for between fifteen and eighteen shillings, depending on the binding (in modern terms, from about $150 to $180). Twenty Shakespeare plays of the thirty-seven that survive first appeared in quarto, seventeen of which appeared during Shakespeare's lifetime; the rest of the plays are found only in folio.

The First Folio was published in 1623, seven years after Shakespeare's death, and was authorized by his fellow actors, the co-owners of the King's Men. This publication was certainly a mark of the company's enormous respect for Shakespeare; but it was also a way of turning the old plays, most of which were no longer current in the play-house, into ready money (the folio includes only Shakespeare's plays, not his sonnets or other nondramatic verse). Whatever the motives behind the publication of the folio, the texts it preserves constitute the basis for almost all later editions of the playwright's works. The texts, however, differ from those of the earlier quartos, sometimes in minor respects but often significantly – most strikingly in the two texts of *King Lear,* but also in important ways in *Hamlet, Othello,* and *Troilus and Cressida.* (The variants are recorded in the textual notes to each play in the new Pelican series.) The differences in these texts represent, in a sense, the essence of theater: the texts of plays were initially not intended for publication. They were scripts, designed for the actors to perform – the principal life of the play at this period was in performance. And it follows that in Shakespeare's theater the playwright typically had no say either in how his play was performed or in the disposition of his text – he was an employee of the company. The authoritative figures in the theatrical enterprise were the shareholders in the company, who were for the most part the major actors. They decided what plays were to be done; they hired the playwright and often gave him an outline of the play they wanted him to write. Often, too, the play was a collaboration: the company would retain a group of writers, and parcel out the scenes among them. The resulting script was then the property of the company, and the actors would revise it as they saw fit during the course of putting it on stage. The resulting text belonged to the company. The playwright had no rights in it once he had been paid. (This system survives largely intact in the movie industry, and most of the playwrights of Shakespeare's time were as anonymous as most screenwriters are today.) The script could also, of course, continue to change as the tastes of audiences and the requirements of the actors changed. Many – perhaps most – plays were revised when they were reintroduced after any substantial absence from the repertory, or when they were performed by a company different from the one that originally commissioned the play.

Shakespeare was an exceptional figure in this world because he was not only a shareholder and actor in his company, but also its leading playwright – he was literally his own boss. He had, moreover, little interest in the publication of his plays, and even those that appeared during his lifetime with the authorization of the company show no signs of any editorial concern on the part of the author. Theater was, for Shakespeare, a fluid and supremely responsive medium – the very opposite of the great classic canonical text that has embodied his works since 1623.

The very fluidity of the original texts, however, has meant that Shakespeare has always had to be edited. Here is an example of how problematic the editorial project inevitably is, a passage from the most famous speech in *Romeo and Juliet,* Juliet's balcony soliloquy beginning "O Romeo, Romeo, wherefore art thou Romeo?" Since the eighteenth century, the standard modern text has read,

> What's Montague? It is nor hand, nor foot,
> Nor arm, nor face, nor any other part
> Belonging to a man. O be some other name!
> What's in a name? That which we call a rose
> By any other name would smell as sweet.
> (II.2.40–44)

Editors have three early texts of this play to work from, two quarto texts and the folio. Here is how the First Quarto (1597) reads:

> Whats *Mountague?* It is nor band nor foote,
> Nor arme, nor face, nor any other part.
> Whats in a name? That which we call a Rofe,
> By any other name would fmell as fweet:

Here is the Second Quarto (1599):

> Whats *Mountague*? it is nor hand nor foote,
> Nor arme nor face, ô be some other name
> Belonging to a man.
> Whats in a name that which we call a rose,
> By any other word would smell as sweete,

And here is the First Folio (1623):

> What's *Mountague*? it is nor hand nor foote,
> Nor arme, nor face, O be some other name
> Belonging to a man.
> What? in a names that which we call a Rose,
> By any other word would smell as sweete,

There is in fact no early text that reads as our modern text does – and this is the most famous speech in the play. Instead, we have three quite different texts, all of which are clearly some version of the same speech, but none of which seems to us a final or satisfactory version. The transcendently beautiful passage in modern editions is an editorial invention: editors have succeeded in conflating and revising the three versions into something we recognize as great poetry. Is this what Shakespeare "really" wrote? Who can say? What we can say is that Shakespeare always had performance, not a book, in mind.

Books About the Shakespeare Texts

The standard study of the printing history of the First Folio is W. W. Greg, *The Shakespeare First Folio* (1955). J. K. Walton, *The Quarto Copy for the First Folio of Shakespeare* (1971), is a useful survey of the relation of the quartos to the folio. The second edition of Charlton Hinman's *Norton Facsimile* of the First Folio (1996), with a new introduction by Peter Blayney, is indispensable. Stanley Wells and Gary Taylor, *William Shakespeare: A Textual Companion*, keyed to the Oxford text, gives a comprehensive survey of the editorial situation for all the plays and poems.

THE GENERAL EDITORS

Introduction

SHAKESPEARE PROBABLY wrote his *Tragedy of Coriolanus* in 1607-8. The play may have been acted for the first time in 1609-10 in the Blackfriars Theatre in London. That indoor theater, supplementing the Globe as an acting venue for the King's Men, the theater company to which Shakespeare belonged, had been leased by the company in 1608 for winter performances. No certainty exists, however, about the exact date of the play's composition, about the time and place of its first performance, or about its initial reception.

In subsequent literary and theatrical history, *Coriolanus* has not become one of Shakespeare's most popular or familiar plays. That is no accident, since the play is centered on a tragic character who, in the name of integrity, courts unpopularity and despises any attempt at crowd-pleasing. As the main character goes, so goes the play. None of the major characters in *Coriolanus* nor the harsh Roman world it represents is particularly appealing. Yet this "cold" play is passionate, coherent, and intellectually gripping. Both the antisocial aggressiveness and emotional withholding of the main character, Coriolanus, make him a fascinatingly perverse charismatic figure. He holds the attention even of characters in the play and of theater audiences who detest him. Shakespeare's presentation of an unsympathetic leading character seems like a complex challenge both to himself as a generally pleasing playwright and to theater audiences who generally like to be pleased.

The unpopular *Coriolanus* isn't wholly atypical among Shakespeare's plays written after 1600. *Hamlet, Measure for Measure, Troilus and Cressida,* and *Timon of Athens,* for example, are all intellectually demanding, and all betray some discomfort on Shakespeare's part with the ordinary conditions of popular playwriting. Both Shakespeare and his playwright contemporary Ben Jonson dramatized their anxiety about the insatiable appetite and grossness of the popular audience as well as their unease about the intellectual concessions involved in catering to it. Yet it is probably in *Coriolanus* that Shakespeare most fully exposes that anxiety. In it, the hunger of Rome's populace during a grain shortage seems like more than just an appetite for bread. From the standpoint of one of Coriolanus's allies, at any rate, it appears that the populace would like to devour Coriolanus. The issue of popular versus unpopular values and personalities is as vexed in Shakespeare's culture as it is in the Roman world he represents. Let us begin, however, by considering *Coriolanus* as a play about Rome before moving on to consider it in its own historical context and in later ones.

Shakespeare based his *Coriolanus* mainly on the "Life of Caius Martius Coriolanus," written in Greek by the historian and essayist Plutarch in C.E. 2, and first translated into English by Sir Thomas North in 1579. (Shakespeare appears to have used the 1595 edition of North's frequently reprinted translation.) Some additional Latin and English sources for the play, the Roman historian Livy's important *History of Rome* among them, have been identified by scholars.

Shakespeare's interest in Roman history is typical of the Renaissance era in which he lived. Many of his playwright contemporaries shared that interest, including the learned Ben Jonson, who wrote the Roman tragedies *Sejanus* and *Catiline.* For members of the Latin-educated intellectual elite of Renaissance Europe, Roman political and cultural models remained the supremely compelling ones inherited from the ancient classical world. Their application to the present was a matter of consuming interest. Leading Renaissance thinkers like Niccolò Machiavelli and Michel de Montaigne made reflections on Roman history the basis both of political theory and of moral philosophy. Yet one did not have to be an advanced Latin scholar or a historian (Shakespeare was neither) to be well informed about Rome, and to feel the force of Roman precedents in daily life. The performance on the Elizabethan stage of plays about Rome, written by Shakespeare and some of his fellow dramatists, made Rome contemporaneous.

The Rome of *Coriolanus* is in its early republican days following the expulsion of the tyrannical king Tarquin. The newly republican Rome of Shakespeare's *Coriolanus* thus differs from the dying republican Rome of his *Julius Caesar* and the budding imperial Rome of his *Antony and Cleopatra,* for both of which Plutarch is also the primary source. It differs as well from the Rome at the end of its imperial days in his *Titus Andronicus.* Although Shakespeare did not write his Roman plays in this historical order – the sequence of composition is *Titus Andronicus* (1593-94), *Julius Caesar* (1599), *Antony and Cleopatra* (1606-7), *Coriolanus* (1607-8) – his interest in particular charged moments and personalities in Roman history seems to have been conditioned throughout his career by an interest in the broad arc of Roman history, from the city's early days to its imperial twilight.

Within this big frame, the Rome of *Coriolanus* is not much more than a city-state at war with the nearby rival city-state of Antium, home of the Volscians. We learn that the hero for whom the play is named had distinguished himself in the war against Tarquin before going on to a glorious military career as Rome's leading warrior. In the play, we see Coriolanus almost single-handedly defeat the Volscians at Corioles, the action that earns him the name "Coriolanus" as an honorific addition to his given names Caius Martius. A military hero to all Romans, and politically favored by the aristocracy (patricians), Coriolanus is nevertheless feared and distrusted by the populace (plebeians), which he openly despises. Coriolanus's conflict with the populace, whose approval he must gain if he is to become a consul, precipitates the tragedy. He believes himself entitled to this political honor on the merit of his military service to the state.

More particularly, we learn in the play that Coriolanus must be approved for the consulship by both the patricians in the senate and the populace in the marketplace. Affirming Coriolanus's worthiness before the senate, Cominius, his military superior and sponsor, launches into an epic recital of Coriolanus's deeds from the time his military career began:

> At sixteen years,
> When Tarquin made a head for Rome, he fought
> Beyond the mark of others. Our then dictator,
> Whom with all praise I point at, saw him fight,
> When with his Amazonian chin he drove
> The bristled lips before him. He bestrid
> An o'erpressed Roman and i' th' consul's view
> Slew three opposers. Tarquin's self he met,
> And struck him on his knee. In that day's feats,
> When he might act the woman in the scene,
> He proved best man i' th' field, and for his meed
> Was brow-bound with the oak.
>
> (II.2.86-97)

In a sense, this recital is unnecessary. The facts are well known to the senators, who do not need to be persuaded of Coriolanus's worthiness. The theater audience has already seen Coriolanus in action against Rome's rivals, so it hardly needs to be convinced of Coriolanus's military prowess. The occasion in the senate, however, becomes one for a formal reaffirmation of the virtues of the military hero, defender of Rome and scourge of its enemies. Cominius's long speech, from which only a brief excerpt is quoted above, also helps to frame the big issues of the play.

The story Cominius tells makes Coriolanus, in the first instance, one of the founding heroes of the Roman republic, conspicuous in the expulsion of King Tarquin and his further defeat when he seeks to reconquer Rome. Yet the adolescent Coriolanus earns his oaken garland at least partly for having protected a fallen Roman comrade on the battlefield. This award signifies the value placed on each citizen by the republic, and emphasizes the importance of comradeship as well as conquest or individual achievement in the republican code. Nevertheless, these images of Coriolanus as a military prodigy reveal Rome's definitively competitive, masculinist, martial values. As the apparently prodigious incarnation of these values, Coriolanus becomes an object of intense desire and admiration to the Roman male elite.

In Cominius's narrative, elite masculinity is proved – both tested and demonstrated – on the field of honor, and is the object of the culture's highest praise. "Act[ing] the woman" is correspondingly disdained; to be a weak man is, in effect, to be a woman. Indeed, the English term "virtue," derived from Latin *vir, virtus* (man, manliness), still bears the imprint of a Roman code that equates moral excellence with heroic masculinity. The one apparently glorious function of women in Shakespeare's represented Rome is to bear warrior sons. When we first meet Volumnia and Virgilia, Coriolanus's mother and wife, they have been summoned to visit another woman, who "lies in" (I.3.77), expecting a child. (Apparently seeking a different route to glory once her son has turned against Rome, however, Volumnia becomes the applauded savior of the city by persuading the vengeful Coriolanus to spare it, for which concession he pays with his life.) A woman visitor to Coriolanus's mother and wife praises his young son for "mammock[ing]" (I.3.65) a butterfly (that is, tearing it apart), an action in which he shows promise of being as fierce as his father. It is the elitist, martial code affirmed in Cominius's speech that will eventually transform an all-conquering Rome from a small city-state into the center of an empire. Yet Cominius's praise, the loftiness of which seems to make even him uncomfortable, is riddled with ironies and contradictions that provide much of the play's substance.

For example, although the word "dictator" in the previously quoted excerpt refers not to the deposed Tarquin but to the then leader of the Roman armies against Tarquin, its referent remains at least momentarily in suspense. The term seems to refer to Tarquin, yet it refers to the Roman general opposing him. Although "dictator" does not have its full modern force in Shakespeare's English, this suspension of reference associates military leadership, on which the state depends, with tyranny as a permanent threat to the state. The one who defeats Tarquin is also the one who may take his place: the idolized defender of the republic is potentially its hated enemy. Thus while Cominius presents defense of the republic and conquest of its enemies as compatible vocations of the Roman military hero, his own language betrays him: the ghost of the "dictator" haunts the republic. The Roman conqueror who begins by conquering the state's enemies may, through an easy reversal, become the conqueror of Rome. A Rome eventually overtaken by its own militarism – a Roman democracy paying the price, in other words, for its ambivalent tolerance of authoritarian codes – is the subject of Shakespeare's *Julius Caesar* and *Antony and Cleopatra*. In the latter play, Octavius Caesar emerges triumphant from the civil wars following the murder of Julius Caesar to become the first Roman emperor. To overthrow a tyrant is not necessarily to eliminate the structure of command – that is, dictatorship – from the republican state or the political culture.

In Cominius's speech, a conflict between militarist and democratic values thus seems latent right from the republic's foundation. It is Coriolanus who will tragically reveal and succumb to this conflict in the play. Although Coriolanus does not in fact aspire to political dictatorship – he merely supports the patricians as Rome's supposedly best-qualified rulers – he is accused of having wanted to be a dictator when he, ironically following in Tarquin's footsteps, is driven out of the city. Coriolanus always wishes to be his own man, yet he never ceases to be trapped in contradictions that are those of the city, not ones of his own making.

The ironies of Coriolanus's predicament in the play are intensified by the fact that it was he, as an adolescent boy wonder, who "struck [Tarquin] on his knee." Coriolanus thus gets significant credit for incapacitating the tyrant, yet that overthrow, as a result of which political power becomes dispersed in the republican state, seems to leave behind it both a power vacuum and an ethical crisis that Coriolanus above all cannot endure. Coriolanus fears that a divided, weakened authority will succumb to popular "confusion" (III.1.109) – the patricians proving too irresolute to exercise power as a class – while truth itself will succumb to a multiplicity of contending voices and hypocritical pretenses. Convinced that neither virtue nor truth is common or popular, and that any attempt to make them appear so can only be false, Coriolanus is ironically condemned to follow in the expelled Tarquin's footsteps, seen as a proud enemy of the people.

In contrast to Coriolanus, the compromising senator Menenius Agrippa tries to articulate a post-despotic vision of the city as an integral body politic – that is to say, as a social organism corresponding to the natural body – with a benign senate as the belly dispensing nutrition to all the limbs and organs. Menenius contradicts his own witty and deliberately charming fable of the body, however, by also speaking, as a patrician, of an abstract, superhuman Roman state indifferent to the citizenry and possessed of its own irresistible momentum: "[Its] course will on / The way it takes, cracking ten thousand curbs" (I.1.67-68). Political models and wills thus clash in the play, while patrician and plebeian classes struggle for dominance. The tribunes, officials newly instituted in Rome to represent the people, give legitimacy to popular power as distinct from the legitimacy already enjoyed by the senatorial aristocracy. In this situation of divided rule, unavoidable compromise, and multiple voices (a term that also means "votes" in the play), it is Coriolanus alone who experiences an almost metaphysical anguish. He always wishes for an undivided authority – and for uncompromised truth –

that seems, ironically, to have perished along with hated political absolutism. In the play's field of philosophical debate, Aufidius, Coriolanus's great warrior opponent, is a relativist, arguing that virtues are never stable or absolute, but "[lie] in th' interpretation of the time" (IV.7.50).

By turns, Coriolanus's craving for the absolute makes him seem like a monster of human pride, counterfeiting deity; like the play's solitary ethical hero; like a traitor to Rome rather than its moral ideal; like the person more deeply compromised in the end than anyone else; or like the eternally naive boy wonder, outmaneuvered by worldly-wise adults, including his mother. For a time, the Volscian hero Aufidius seems like Coriolanus's double in the play, yet repeated defeats disillusion him, making him willing to destroy Coriolanus by deceit if need be. This corruption of the Volscian hero is what enables him to win in the grown-up world of the play. Indeed, it is the taunt "boy" (V.6.100) from Aufidius at the end of the play that brings Coriolanus's history full circle and inflames him to a rage at once murderous and suicidal. Completely isolated in Corioles, as he was in Rome, he is cut to pieces by the Volscians whose cause he has supported.

Coriolanus seems wholly unfitted for republican politics. Indeed, his inability to compromise virtually defines the Roman political sphere by contrast *as* one of compromise and moderation. His self-isolating and self-destructive folly, obvious to everyone in the play, makes it hard for anyone to sympathize with him. He views himself as a "lonely dragon" (IV.1.30) when he is about to be expelled from Rome, yet he has brought this solitude on himself by his railing abrasiveness and unconcealed disdain for the populace; by his conviction of his own merit; by his (seemingly affected) humility in relation to an internalized standard of absolute value; and by his disruptive refusal of any workable political or social compromise. His lack of self-control makes it possible for the Roman tribunes to manipulate him almost at will, to his own undoing. Schooled in the Roman wars, Coriolanus apparently cannot adapt to the world of Roman politics; his rigidity makes him almost more comic than tragic.

Yet Coriolanus cannot easily be dismissed. Not only do the Romans depend on his military prowess, but he is never more passionately, proudly Roman – never more expressive of Roman core values – than when he is at odds with the city of his birth. He evidently *chooses* not to adapt. Referring to the plebeians, he says, "I had rather be their servant in my way, / Than sway [rule] with them in theirs" (II.1.198-99). He would far rather use language as a weapon than as an instrument of conciliation, and finds his voice in doing so. (When he greets his wife as "my gracious silence" [II.1.171], he is implicitly equating silence with demure feminine weakness, and is seeing her as his own feminine alter ego.) His hard, brilliant, cutting eloquence, echoed elsewhere in the play, is a language of antisocial satire. Indeed, Coriolanus is never happier, and never feels more fully vindicated, than when he stands at bay, assailed by everyone around him (a situation in which he repeatedly places himself, starting with the battle at Corioles). His preferred form of social interaction in Rome is the paradoxical one of aggressive bonding with the very plebeians he disdains. He goes out of his way to offend and berate them; the play's shrewd, articulate plebeians give as good as they get. This jarring confrontation between opposites, repeatedly provoked by Coriolanus, is feared by all the play's negotiators and manipulators, from Menenius and the tribunes through Volumnia and Virgilia. They intervene successfully, in the city's political interests as well as their own. Yet a strangely intense, contradictory attraction underlies Coriolanus's antipathy toward his plebeian opposites. When he speaks disdainfully of them as his collective "sworn brother" (II.3.95), the irony may be deeper than he realizes. Curses may bind as well as vows.

A famous ironic exchange between Menenius and the tribune Sicinius also draws attention to something more complicated than pure antagonism in the city's polarized social relations:

> SICINIUS Nature teaches beasts to know their
> friends.
> MENENIUS Pray you, who does the wolf love?
> SICINIUS The lamb.
> MENENIUS Ay, to devour him, as the hungry ple-
> beians would the noble Martius.
>
> (II.1.6-10)

Powerful yet destructive forms of appetite and perverse at-
tachment are hinted at in the play's allusions to starvation
and cannibalism, neither of which is purely literal despite
the famine raging in the city when the play opens. As the
philosopher Stanley Cavell noted in *Disowning Knowledge,* Shakespeare's "who does the wolf love?" can mean
either "whom does the wolf love?" or "who loves the
wolf?" The lamb may love its devourer and vice versa. It is
this plane of contradictory passion and predatory interchange
that Coriolanus prefers to the milder civic one still
emerging in republican Rome.

The political condition of Coriolanus and the Rome he
inhabits is reflected and elaborated on the familial and personal levels. Since the figure of the absolute monarch is that
of the father (paterfamilias) writ large, Tarquin's overthrow
is also the symbolic overthrow of an absolute paternal
power. In the void thus created, Coriolanus's mother, Volumnia, emerges as a figure of overpowering domination
and of women's continuing frustration. Although Menenius Agrippa sentimentally claims to be a father to Coriolanus when he wishes to persuade him not to conquer
Rome, and although Menenius tries to persuade the plebeians that the senators are the city's good fathers, there are
really no powerful fathers in the play; even Coriolanus's
young son revolts against him. "He did it to please his
mother" (I.1.36-37), a citizen shrewdly notes about Coriolanus's military exploits. Volumnia, who is strongly identified with Rome yet confined to domesticity and unable to
participate in its political life or military glories, has deliberately shaped Coriolanus as her surrogate in the world of

male action. In wishing him to stand for the consulship, which he says he does not want although he feels entitled to it, she is making him her surrogate in the Roman political world as well as the military one. As she says, her son takes the place of a strong husband in her life. She whiles away domestic time in the play by fantasizing Coriolanus's encounter in battle with his Volscian opponent, Aufidius. Coriolanus's death in battle would redound to Volumnia's credit and feed her desire no less than do his military triumphs. Indeed, her permanent, consuming rage at being excluded ("Anger's my meat," IV.2.50) leads one to suspect that she might prefer Coriolanus as a dead male hero to Coriolanus as a living one. Tellingly, it is she, not he, who becomes the savior of Rome in the end, at the cost of his life. As he says to her after she has fatally persuaded him to relent, "O mother, mother! / What have you done?" (V.3.182-83). Apparently the overthrow of the tyrannical "father" in a system of continuing male privilege and identification results in the rise not of the powerful matriarch but of the ferocious anti-mother. The eclipse of the "father" also makes it difficult, perhaps impossible, for the Roman hero to identify himself as he wishes.

In Sigmund Freud's classic psychoanalytic theory, the normal scenario for masculine identity formation is the oedipal one. The son who symbolically kills his lawgiving father does so in order to take his place, thus securing his own identity. This scenario, which Freud deduced principally from Shakespeare's *Hamlet* (1600-1), is preempted in *Coriolanus* (1607-8), however, since, in the republic, Coriolanus cannot take the place of the outlawed Tarquin. What is left behind after the expulsion of Tarquin is a void that Coriolanus is forbidden to occupy. Still psychically inhabiting a structure of paternal absolutism, yet shaped by a domineering mother, Coriolanus possesses no masculine identity except the one he tries to create for himself in action. This situation of lack drives him to hypermasculine extremes, ones that always seem more like a flight from the feminine, however, than positively masculine. His adult self-formation, lacking any positive model or legitimizing structure, is virtually doomed to be negative, contradictory, and finally impossible (this too is implied when Aufidius taunts him as "boy").

Various critics have observed that when Coriolanus emerges triumphant after a seemingly suicidal lone sortie into the besieged city of Corioles, his blood-bathed body looks almost like one new-born in battle. It is as if, to be a man, the "fatherless" Coriolanus must be reborn of his own volition in the masculine setting of war. This "rebirth" separates him from the feminine identity still implied in Cominius's allusion to his "Amazonian [i.e., hairless] chin" when a young man. The precocious boy soldier evidently looks more like a woman warrior than a man. Repeated separation from the feminine, which apparently includes the entire domestic sphere of marriage and family life, is the option provided by the all-male Roman military career, pursued in a place apart from the home. This career allows masculine independence to be pursued, and heroic masculine identity to be formed, in ferocious rivalry yet also bonded intimacy with a warrior enemy. Even more than passionate comradeship, displayed on occasion by Coriolanus, repeated encounters with the enemy champion appear to provide the highest satisfaction for both Coriolanus and Aufidius, at least until Coriolanus wins once too often. What animates these ecstatic love-hate relations between enemies (ones Coriolanus apparently seeks to replicate in his relations with the reluctant plebeians) turns out to be a passionate homoerotic attraction given no healthy acknowledgment in Rome's masculine warrior code or its domestic code of heterosexual marriage.

Both the erotic power of the male bond and its displacement of the male-female marriage bond are virtually spelled out in a memorable declaration by Aufidius. When Coriolanus, having been banished from Rome (or having banished it, as he prefers to think!), proposes that they join forces to destroy Rome, Aufidius replies,

> Know thou first,
> I loved the maid I married; never man
> Sighed truer breath. But that I see thee here,
> Thou noble thing, more dances my rapt heart
> Than when I first my wedded mistress saw
> Bestride my threshold.
>
> . . . .
>
> Thou hast beat me out
> Twelve several times, and I have nightly since
> Dreamt of encounters 'twixt thyself and me.
> We have been down together in my sleep,
> Unbuckling helms, fisting each other's throat,
> And waked half dead with nothing.
>
> (IV.5.117-30)

"We have been down together" has been glossed to mean
that Aufidius has dreamt of violent wrestling bouts with
Coriolanus, but that gloss clearly understates the nature
of this orgasmic dream encounter. If we are tempted to
call both this sadomasochistic fantasy and the masculine
warrior culture that has produced it pathological, we
should nevertheless recall that the payoff from it in the
political arena is power and conquest. It is on this unac-
knowledged – indeed, repressed and deflected – male ho-
moeroticism that the state builds.

As a mechanism for producing elite masculine identity,
rivalrous bonding between men is subject to its own dis-
contents. On one hand, it produces no distinct, stable
identity but only a fleeting mirror image of the self. It is
ironic that none of the Volscians, not even Aufidius, rec-
ognizes the great Coriolanus when he arrives in Corioles
in mean attire, not looking like "himself." On the other
hand, rivalrous bonding succumbs to both repetition and
inequality. As the repeated loser, Aufidius becomes poisoned with envy, forfeiting self-respect. As the repeated
winner, Coriolanus aspires to rise above rivalry altogether,
gaining an absolute identity owed to no other person.

Throughout the play, Coriolanus's desire for transcendent identity, hence self-sufficiency, is revealed by his suspicion of any names given to him except the one he has earned; of any form of praise; or of any recognition conferred on him by any other. The idea that he has to depend on the plebeians' goodwill in order to become a consul is abhorrent to him. Although he claims that his reluctance to expose his war wounds in public comes from modesty, their exposure would in fact reveal the vulnerable human body, and perhaps a "feminine" capacity to bleed, belying his armored male self. In Shakespeare's *Julius Caesar,* the wounded, exposed body of the murdered dictator, which moves the crowd to tears, "feminizes" both him and them.

After he has left Rome and gained even greater advantage over Aufidius, as an ally than as a rival, Coriolanus is seen by the Roman men who come to plead with him as a singularly remote, invulnerable, self-sufficient being approaching the condition of a god. The Roman men see him that way partly because they continue to project their own fantasies onto Coriolanus. Coriolanus at his most exalted refuses to speak the language of human recognition, relatedness, and exchange, thus virtually removing himself from humanity altogether. Cominius reports,

> Yet one time he did call me by my name.
> I urged our old acquaintance, and the drops
> That we have bled together. "Coriolanus"
> He would not answer to, forbade all names.
> He was a kind of nothing, titleless,
> Till he had forged himself a name o' th' fire
> Of burning Rome.
>
> (V.1.9-15)

Aristotle remarked that the one who lives alone is either a god or a beast. Although this aphorism has often been quoted in connection with Coriolanus, the point is made more metaphysically here by Shakespeare: the one all alone is either a god or nothing. To be a god in human guise is to be nobody at all, since humanity is constituted only in relation to other humans, and by their recognition.

Although Coriolanus, wishing to be immovable, forbids further emissaries from Rome once he has heard the pleas of Cominius and Menenius, his mother, wife, son, and a woman friend somehow break through the cordon to plead with him. Confronted by those whose relationships to him he cannot deny, Coriolanus's absoluteness crumbles. The bravado of his declaration "Wife, mother, child, I know not" (V.2.78) proves unsustainable. Indeed, when he must face the women who plead for Rome – the three V's, Volumnia, Virgilia, and Valeria – the hopelessness of attempted male flight from the feminine also becomes evident: they confront him like his own fates. Therefore this verbal showdown, in which Coriolanus caves in after the dramatic buildup in which he has threatened Rome with destruction, constitutes one of the greatest prolonged anticlimaxes in dramatic history. It will be followed by the further anticlimax of Coriolanus's virtually suicidal death, the only way out of human relatedness.

Both Coriolanus's capitulation to Volumnia and the sudden hysteria, falsity, and confusion of the speeches he makes in his rediscovered roles as son, husband, father, and friend imply that his quest for uncompromised identity and absolute separation has been illusory all along. Although Coriolanus is not simply taken in by the voluminous rhetoric of family obligation Volumnia delivers in this scene – he seems unsure whether he is being overcome by natural "instinct" (V.3.35) or by her manipulation – he is nonetheless being confronted by the "mortal" (V.3.189) inescapability of his human connections. They can neither be denied nor fled. Shakespeare's critique of Coriolanus's aspiration is decisive.

So much, then, for *Coriolanus* as a play about ancient Rome, albeit a Rome still recognized as a shaping force in Shakespeare's political culture. Despite Shakespeare's reliance on classical sources, some modern scholars have chosen to treat *Coriolanus* not as a play about Rome but either as a direct reflection of English political life at the time it was written or as Shakespeare's projection of his own cultural world into ancient Rome. This critical strategy has been productive, although it has sometimes been pursued without enough regard to the uncertain boundary between past and present in Shakespeare's work, or to broad cultural continuities spanning historical differences. Subject to those qualifications, let us now turn briefly to the question of *Coriolanus* in its own time.

Critics who treat Coriolanus as a play about seventeenth-century England do not necessarily presume that Shakespeare was ignorant of Roman history or indifferent to historical accuracy. Transposing contemporary history into ancient Rome might have been his way of gaining perspective on it. Moreover, given the riskiness of direct political commentary in autocratic, seventeenth-century England, Shakespeare would not have been the only writer to deal obliquely with contemporary issues by presenting them as Roman ones. What seems clear, however, is that Shakespeare's presentation of Rome in *Coriolanus* is conditioned not just by contemporary politics but by broadly held contemporary beliefs in various fields, and by his own vocational interests as an actor and playwright. He freely alters or supplements Plutarch in accordance with his own concerns.

Some commentators have suggested that Shakespeare reads Roman culture as more patriarchal than it may have been, thus projecting onto ancient Rome the strongly patriarchal mind-set of his own time. Although the issue is difficult to resolve, the claim gains credibility with respect to *Coriolanus* from the fact that during the reign of James I, who came to power following the death of the popular Queen Elizabeth I in 1603, a patriarchal, absolutist ideal of the state, sanctioned by Roman precedents, was promoted by the royal court. A consciously withdrawn, "unpopular," antitheatrical political style at once justified and reinforced James I's personal unpopularity as successor to

Elizabeth I. *Coriolanus* does not just reflect these historical facts but explores some of the interconnected political, psychological, and cultural implications of absolutism. Whether as an immediate political reality or as a threatening ghost, absolutism is a central concern not just of *Coriolanus* and the other Roman plays, but of *Macbeth* and *King Lear*. Critics continue to debate whether Shakespeare identifies himself with absolutism or resists it, yet the plays suggest he does both: the phenomenon is too interesting as well as threatening, too multidimensional, and too deeply embedded in his culture for him simply to take sides.

The factional conflicts of *Coriolanus*, although sufficiently grounded in Plutarch, reveal the tensions of an English state increasingly polarized between royal absolutism and parliamentary republicanism, and increasingly threatened by popular insurrection. The threat of plebeian revolt brought on by famine in *Coriolanus* probably alludes to popular uprisings, resulting from recurrent food shortages and high prices, in the English midlands (including Shakespeare's home county of Warwickshire) during 1607-8. Yet the threat of popular insurrection in *Coriolanus* – and increasingly in seventeenth-century England – is not confined to peasant revolt in a feudal world. The plebeians in *Coriolanus* are tradesmen finding their voices in an urban political milieu and gaining formal representation through their newly appointed tribunes. Even if this gain exposes them to manipulation by their own representatives, it ratifies their power as a class.

Unlike the plebeians in *Julius Caesar*, those in *Coriolanus* are acute observers and critics of their political world, who cogently discuss both the political issues and Coriolanus's character. They do not find power inscrutable. Their accusation that the patricians are hoarding grain to drive up its price is never convincingly refuted in the play. Nor do any facts refute their charge that the rich have an interest in maintaining poverty, since wealth exists only in contrast to poverty, not all on its own. A historical transmutation of peasant revolt into urban political radicalism is implied in

Coriolanus; such urban radicalism, antihierarchical and sometimes communistic, would become politically important during the English Civil War (1642-49).

Some of the best recent scholarship on *Coriolanus* has connected the play in detail to seventeenth-century English political debate. Many of the specific terms of dispute between James I and the English Parliament about royal entitlements are repeated in the play. Big, traditional political metaphors, like that of the body politic, get reworked, not just in Menenius's speech, but throughout the play. Yet the issues of *Coriolanus* are not just immediate ones of the decade in which it was written. The language of English political life was being fundamentally reformulated during the reign of James I, despite the appearance of feudal continuity in English social relations and political rhetoric.

The term "early modern" is now often applied to the historical period of *Coriolanus*, and many twentieth-century readers have been struck by the modernity of the political vocabulary and lines of division in *Coriolanus*. Indeed, the play has seemed so prophetic – or so current – that it has been connected to practically every political cause or source of anxiety in the twentieth century, in England, Europe, and the United States. It has been regarded as speaking directly to issues ranging from proletarian revolution and fascism in the 1930s and 1940s, through conservative versus socialist politics in the period after World War II, to Nicaragua and Iran-Contra in the 1980s and 1990s. This list is far from complete. In the play's performance history in this century it was – to focus on only one remarkable sequence noted by R. B. Parker, one of the play's most recent editors – first banned by the Nazis as a radio play and then adopted by them as a school text; banned by the American occupation forces in postwar Germany; and rewritten in the service of the proletariat by the German playwright Bertolt Brecht, in a version he was still working on at the time of his death in 1956.

Onstage, the portrayal of Coriolanus has veered between positive and negative extremes, depending on whether authoritarian or democratic, fascist or revolutionary interests were primarily being served. So numerous, in fact, have major, politically committed productions of *Coriolanus* been in this century that R. B. Parker felt driven to classify them en masse as either left wing or right wing. Insofar as "politics" has increasingly come to mean "sexual politics" in recent years, *Coriolanus* has been caught up in that transition, lending itself to both feminist and queer interpretation ("leather" performances of *Coriolanus* had already begun in the 1970s). The continuing provocativeness of the play attests to the long-term effect of political changes that took place during the seventeenth century, but it attests just as much to the enduring effect of early modern cultural formations.

Both the sexual politics and the identity politics of *Coriolanus* appear to be grounded in early modern conceptions of sexuality and gender. Although traditional philosophy gave some support to the notion that men and women belong to so-called opposite sexes, what appears to have been equally influential during the early modern period, also inherited from classical antiquity, was a one-sex theory that made men and women physiological mirror images of one another. According to the researcher Thomas Laqueur in *Making Sex,* women's sexual organs were regarded as internalized versions of men's sexual organs (vagina and ovaries corresponding to penis and testes) and vice versa; bodies were drawn that way in anatomy textbooks. Sexual identity and difference were therefore not necessarily considered to be grounded in absolute bodily difference.

In the absence of mutually exclusive opposite sexes, a range of sexualities became conceivable, and these were indeed acted out on the Elizabethan stage, on which boys generally played women's parts. Furthermore, the notion that men's and women's sexual anatomies are exclusively fitted to one another, as key is to lock, was challenged during the Renaissance by Leonardo da Vinci among others. Widespread homosexual practices belied the supposition that men exclusively penetrate while women are exclusively penetrated in the sexual act.

Cultural fears about gender indeterminacy in the absence of absolute sexual differences meant that masculine sexual identification came to depend either on secondary traits like beardedness, or on clothing, social roles, and self-presentation. All these signs of sexual identity proved unreliable, however, since they either could be duplicated as forms of disguise or could fail to produce absolute distinctions. The weird sisters in *Macbeth* are bearded. Shakespeare's comic heroines masquerade successfully as young men. The young Coriolanus looks like an Amazon. Beardless male adolescents seemingly have to make a difficult transition, not just from boyhood to manhood, but from womanhood to manhood. The reversibility of that progression is implied by the fact that Coriolanus feels as if he is turning back into a little boy and/or a woman (the two being virtually equivalent in his mind) whenever he is asked to compromise:

> Away, my disposition, and possess me
> Some harlot's spirit! My throat of war be turned,
> Which quired with my drum, into a pipe
> Small as an eunuch, or the virgin voice
> That babies lulls asleep!

> (III.2.111–15)

Such anxieties (and the virulent misogyny accompanying them) simply could not have existed had people believed that the male identity they valued so highly was securely grounded in sexual anatomy. In other words, masculine sexual identity was crucially a product of continuing social performance. By the same token, absolute male identity, whether pursued in military action or in any other way, remained both groundless and unattainable under Renaissance assumptions, for which reason its pursuit could become tragically obsessive, as it does in *Coriolanus* and *Macbeth*.

By preference, Coriolanus pursues manhood as well as his absolute "truth" in a world of pure male action. When he is asked to compromise politically in Rome, and to present himself in the public arena to the plebeians, he feels not only that he is becoming a woman – hence, by easy extension in his mind, a whore – but that he is being turned into a mere actor as well. Indeed, Volumnia shares the latter understanding, yet accepts it, insisting on becoming Coriolanus's drama coach in the popular performance required of him:

> I prithee now, my son,
> Go to them, with this bonnet in thy hand;
> And thus far having stretched it – here be with
> them –
> Thy knee bussing the stones – for in such business
> Action is eloquence, and the eyes of th' ignorant
> More learned than the ears – waving thy head,
>
> . . . .
>
> say to them
> Thou art their soldier.

(III.2.72–81)

What seems to Coriolanus most compromising of all to personal virtue and truth is acting a part. To be possessed of true identity is simply to be oneself in action; acting implies either a lack or a loss of authentic being. The fact that Coriolanus's mother insists he perform, and shows unexpected expertise in coaching him, compromises her in his eyes; he is also shocked by her sudden substitution of a new, deceiving play script for the seemingly authentic script of manhood she has previously fed him. He cannot refute her argument that he already accepts deception as a part of military strategy, yet he feels radically unsettled by her sudden change of front. Protecting his masculine identity and integrity becomes definitively aligned in his mind with a violent antitheatricality. For him, harlot and actor become practically the same thing. In the end, Coriolanus refuses to become an actor in the political theater of Rome, and is violently expelled from the city – indeed he is hooted out of it in disgrace, having failed to perform.

At one level, Coriolanus's antitheatricality belongs to the period in which the play was written. The *performance* of masculine sovereignty was repudiated by James I as the somewhat hapless male successor to the highly theatrical and charismatically successful Elizabeth I, yet that form of antitheatricality was pervasive in the masculine, absolutist cultures of seventeenth-century Europe as well. At another level, the antitheatrical prejudice, as the critic Jonas Barish named it in his book published under that title, seems to have been endemic in Western culture from the earliest times. If so, it belongs, culturally speaking, both to ancient Rome and seventeenth-century England. Insofar as masculine integrity, identity, and truth persist as core cultural values, both misogyny and antitheatricality readily follow from them. Shakespeare's relation to those core values was bound to be ambivalent, since he was both an actor and a playwright, vocationally committed to the socializing values of performance. That ambivalence is very deeply marked in *Coriolanus*. Yet *Coriolanus* also implies that those core values all too often play out tragically, and that an escape from role-playing is impossible.

Coriolanus's career really ends when he finds himself, in the decisive confrontation of the play, caught onstage in a performance controlled by his mother, not facing a male opponent: "Like a dull actor now, / I have forgot my part, and I am out, / Even to a full disgrace" (V.3.40-42). Even though, in the fictional world of the play, Coriolanus's encounter with his family is not literally occurring on a stage, he sees it as a performance being witnessed by an audience of gods, whom he imagines laughing rather than weeping at the "unnatural scene" (V.3.184). Coriolanus had thought he could leave the great political theater of Rome behind him when, at his expulsion from the city, he had declared "There is a world elsewhere" (III.3.136), yet he finds that there is no such world. Rome follows him, just as he compulsively comes back to it for his revenge. (In *Julius Caesar,* Shakespeare puns "Rome" with "room," the latter term referring to the empty space of the theater, but also to a Rome that has by then made all the world its stage, leaving no imaginable "world elsewhere.") If Coriolanus is defeated in the play, it is less by his rival Aufidius than by the Roman contradictions in which he is forever enmeshed.

While the Romans are understandably grateful to Volumnia for having saved their city, and while one can hardly wish that Coriolanus had burned Rome (his own family along with the "chaff" [V.1.26] from which, he says, it would be too much trouble to sort them out), Volumnia's triumph at Coriolanus's expense is an unhappy one. It leaves us with little to celebrate, and attests to deep cultural rifts that the play is more successful at revealing than resolving. Yet the play is one of unsentimental clarity and exciting intellectual rigor. Although Coriolanus never enjoys the monopoly of truth he craves (nobody in the play does, though practically everyone speaks it tellingly on occasion), he puts truth on the line, and the play abundantly delivers it, even when it does so at his expense. Despite its relative unpopularity, the brilliant and challenging *Coriolanus* has paradoxically remained a major Shakespearean play in performance throughout this century, still making Rome contemporaneous.

JONATHAN CREWE
Dartmouth College

Note on the Text

THE TRAGEDY OF CORIOLANUS was first published in the 1623 folio edition of Shakespeare's plays. The present edition follows that text. The folio *Coriolanus* is divided into acts but not scenes. The scene divisions in this text are ones proposed over time by various editors and adopted in the previous Pelican edition of the play. The main difficulty presented by the folio text concerns line division in blank verse passages. Lineation seems incorrect or irregular in an unusually large number of cases. No proposed correction or regularization is wholly satisfactory, and a strong argument can be made for leaving well enough alone, as I have done in nearly every case. Speakers in the play are often designated by generic names, with or without numerals: e.g., *I. Citizen, Senator.* I have generally spelled out such names or supplemented them: e.g., *First Citizen, First Senator.* Substantive departures from the folio text are listed below. The adopted reading appears in italics and is followed by the folio reading in roman.

I.1   55 *FIRST CITIZEN* 2 Cit. (and so through rest of scene)   64 *you. For* you for   90 *stale* scale   108 *tauntingly* taintingly   113 *crownèd* crown'd   182 *vile* vilde   212 *Shouting* Shooting   224 s.d. *Junius* Annius   237 *Lartius* Lucius   242, 246 *First Senator* Sen.

I.2   4 *on* one

I.3   36 *that's* that   83 *Ithaca* Athica   111 s.d. *Exeunt* Exeunt Ladies

I.4   s.d. *[a trumpeter], Drum* Drum   54 *lost* loft

I.5   3 s.d. *Alarum* exeunt. Alarum; *Titus Lartius* Titus

I.6   24 s.d. *Enter Martius* (at l. 21 in F)   32 *burned* burnt   53 *Antiates* Antients   71 *Lesser* Lessen   82 *select* select from all

I.7   7 s.d. *Exeunt* Exit

I.9   46 *coverture* Ouerture   50 *shout* shoot   66 *All* Omnes; *Caius Martius* Marcus Caius   67, 78, 81, 89 *CORIOLANUS* Martius

I.10   2, 16, 29, 33 *FIRST SOLDIER* Sould   22 *Embargements* Embarquements

II.1   17 *with all* withall   55 *cannot* can   59 *you you* you   62 *bisson* beesome   161 *Coriolanus* Martius Caius Coriolanus   185 *relish* Rallish **199 s.d.** *Brutus . . . forward* Enter Brutus and Sicinius **212** *guarded* gawded **250** *touch* teach **255** *to th'* to the

II.2 46 *Caius Martius* Martius Caius **67, 122, 129** FIRST SENATOR Senat **80** *one on's* on ones **90** *chin* Shinne **91** *bristled* brizled **107** *took. From face to foot* tooke from face to foote: **137** *suffrage* sufferage **153** SENATORS Senat **153 s.d.** *Manent* Manet

II.3 27 *wedged* wadg'd **36** *it. I say,* it, I say. If **40** *all together* altogether **60 s.d.** *Enter . . . Citizens* (at l. 59 in F) **66** *not* but **87, 90, 105** FOURTH CITIZEN I. **103** FIFTH CITIZEN 2. **113** *hire* higher **114** *toge* tongue **117** *do't* doo't? **120** *t' o'erpeer* to or'epeere **125, 130** *voices!* voyces? **131** SIXTH first **133** SEVENTH second **226** *th'* the **243** *And [Censorinus] nobly* And nobly; *namèd* nam'd **244** *being [by the people chosen]* being chosen

III.1 s.d. *Lartius* Latius **10** *vilely* vildly **31, 63, 75** FIRST SENATOR Senat. **90** *O good* O God! **142** *Where one* Whereon **171 s.d.** *Enter an Aedile* (at l. 170 in F) **184** ALL (at l. 188 in F) **199, 234, 336** FIRST SENATOR Sena. **232** CORIOLANUS Com. **238** COMINIUS Corio. **239** CORIOLANUS Mene. **289** *Our* One **304** SICINIUS Menen. **324** *bring him* bring him in peace

III.2 13 s.d. *Enter Volumnia* (at l. 6 in F) **21** *taxings* things **26** FIRST SENATOR Sen. **32** *herd* heart **101** *bear? Well, I* beare Well? I **115** *lulls* lull

III.3 32 *for th'* fourth **36** *Throng* Through **55** *accents* Actions **99** *i' th' name* In the Name **110** *for* from **136 s.d.** *Menenius* Cumalijs **138** *Hoo! hoo!* Hoo, oo.

IV.1 34 *wilt* will **37** VIRGILIA Cor.

IV.2 9 s.d. *Enter . . . Menenius* (at l. 7 in F) **36** *let us* let's **44 s.d.** *Exeunt* Exit **53 s.d.** *Exeunt* (at end of preceding speech in F, with *Exit* here)

IV.3 32 *will* well

IV.4 23 *hate* haue

IV.5 111 *thy* that **135** *o'erbear't* oerbeat **154** *strucken* strocken **168** *on* one **183** *lief* liue **209** *sowl* sole **232** *sprightly, waking* spightly walking **234** *sleepy* sleepe **236** *war* warres

IV.6 10 s.d. *Enter Menenius* (at l. 9 in F) **26** CITIZENS All **141** ALL CITIZENS Omnes

IV.7 15 *Had* haue **37** *'twas* 'was **49** *virtues* Vertue **55** *founder* fouler

V.1 41 *toward* towards

V.2 s.d. *on* or **16** *haply* happely **56 s.d.** *and* with **58** *errand* arrant **61** *by my* my **72** *our* your **83** *pity note* pitty: Note **90 s.d.** *Manent* Manet

V.3 48 *prate* pray **56** *What is* What's **63** *holp* hope **79** *you'd* youl'd **149** *fine* fiue **154** *noble man* Nobleman **163** *clucked* clock'd **169** *him* him with him **179** *this* his

V.5 4 *Unshout* Unshoot

V.6 10 *empoisoned* impoisoned **48 s.d.** *sound* sounds **74** *That* Then, **99** *other* others **114** *Fluttered* Flatter'd **115** *it. Boy?* it, Boy. **129 s.d.** *Draw* Draw both; *kill* kils **153 s.d.** *Coriolanus* Martius

Coriolanus

[NAMES OF THE ACTORS

CAIUS MARTIUS, *afterwards Caius Martius Coriolanus*
TITUS LARTIUS ⎫
COMINIUS ⎭ *Generals against the Volscians*
MENENIUS AGRIPPA, *friend to Coriolanus*
VOLUMNIA, *mother to Coriolanus*
VIRGILIA, *wife to Coriolanus*
VALERIA, *friend to Virgilia*
SICINIUS VELUTUS ⎫
JUNIUS BRUTUS ⎭ *Tribunes of the People*
YOUNG MARTIUS, *son to Coriolanus*
NICANOR, *a Roman*
GENTLEWOMAN, *attending on Virgilia*
SENATORS ⎫
OFFICERS ⎪
AEDILES ⎬ *of Rome*
HERALDS ⎪
MESSENGERS ⎪
SOLDIERS ⎭
CITIZENS OF ROME
TULLUS AUFIDIUS, *General of the Volscians*
ADRIAN, *a Volscian*
LIEUTENANT TO AUFIDIUS
CONSPIRATORS WITH AUFIDIUS
SERVANTS TO AUFIDIUS
SENATORS ⎫
LORDS ⎬ *of Corioles*
SOLDIERS ⎭
A CITIZEN OF ANTIUM

SCENE: *Rome and the neighborhood; the Volscian
         towns of Corioles and Antium*]

*

The Tragedy of Coriolanus

❧ **I.1** *Enter a company of mutinous Citizens, with staves, clubs, and other weapons.*

FIRST CITIZEN Before we proceed any further, hear me speak.

ALL Speak, speak.

FIRST CITIZEN You are all resolved rather to die than to famish?

ALL Resolved, resolved.

FIRST CITIZEN First, you know Caius Martius is chief enemy to the people.

ALL We know't, we know't.

FIRST CITIZEN Let us kill him, and we'll have corn at our own price. Is't a verdict? 10 11

ALL No more talking on't! Let it be done! Away, away! 12

SECOND CITIZEN One word, good citizens.

FIRST CITIZEN We are accounted poor citizens, the patricians good. What authority surfeits on would relieve us. If they would yield us but the superfluity while it were wholesome, we might guess they relieved us humanely, but they think we are too dear. The leanness that afflicts us, the object of our misery, is as an inventory to particularize their abundance; our sufferance is a gain to them. Let us revenge this with our pikes ere 15 16 18 19 20 21

I.1 A street in Rome **11** *verdict* agreement **12** *on't* about it **15** *patricians* aristocrats; *good* substantial; *authority* the ruling class; *surfeits* sickens with excess **16** *superfluity* surplus **18** *dear* expensive **19** *object* spectacle **19–20** *inventory . . . abundance* list to detail their contrasting wealth **20** *sufferance* suffering **21** *pikes* pitchforks

22   we become rakes; for the gods know I speak this in
hunger for bread, not in thirst for revenge.

SECOND CITIZEN   Would you proceed especially against
Caius Martius?

26 ALL   Against him first. He's a very dog to the common-
27   alty.

SECOND CITIZEN   Consider you what services he has
done for his country?

30 FIRST CITIZEN   Very well, and could be content to give
him good report for't, but that he pays himself with
being proud.

SECOND CITIZEN   Nay, but speak not maliciously.

FIRST CITIZEN   I say unto you, what he hath done fa-
35   mously, he did it to that end. Though soft-conscienced
men can be content to say it was for his country, he did
it to please his mother and to be partly proud, which he
38   is, even to the altitude of his virtue.

SECOND CITIZEN   What he cannot help in his nature,
40   you account a vice in him. You must in no way say he is
41   covetous.

FIRST CITIZEN   If I must not, I need not be barren of accusations. He hath faults, with surplus, to tire in repetition.

    Shouts within.

What shouts are these? The other side o' th' city is risen.
46   Why stay we prating here? To th' Capitol!

ALL   Come, come!

48 FIRST CITIZEN   Soft, who comes here?

    Enter Menenius Agrippa.

SECOND CITIZEN   Worthy Menenius Agrippa, one that
50   hath always loved the people.

FIRST CITIZEN   He's one honest enough! Would all the
rest were so!

---

22 *rakes* i.e., lean as rakes   26 *very dog* ferocious enemy   **26–27** *commonalty*
common people   35 *to that end* i.e., to achieve fame; *soft-conscienced* weak-
minded   38 *altitude of his virtue* height of his valor   41 *covetous* self-serving
46 *prating* talking idly; *Capitol* Temple of Jupiter, Capitoline Hill   48 *Soft*
stay

MENENIUS
  What work's, my countrymen, in hand? Where go you
  With bats and clubs? The matter? Speak, I pray you.
FIRST CITIZEN   Our business is not unknown to th' Sen-
  ate. They have had inkling this fortnight what we in-
  tend to do, which now we'll show 'em in deeds. They
  say poor suitors have strong breaths; they shall know   58
  we have strong arms too.
MENENIUS
  Why, masters, my good friends, mine honest neighbors,   60
  Will you undo yourselves?
FIRST CITIZEN   We cannot, sir, we are undone already.
MENENIUS
  I tell you, friends, most charitable care
  Have the patricians of you. For your wants,   64
  Your suffering in this dearth, you may as well   65
  Strike at the heaven with your staves as lift them
  Against the Roman state, whose course will on   67
  The way it takes, cracking ten thousand curbs
  Of more strong link asunder than can ever
  Appear in your impediment. For the dearth,   70
  The gods, not the patricians, make it, and
  Your knees to them, not arms, must help. Alack,
  You are transported by calamity   73
  Thither where more attends you, and you slander
  The helms o' th' state, who care for you like fathers,   75
  When you curse them as enemies.
FIRST CITIZEN   Care for us? True, indeed! They ne'er
  cared for us yet: suffer us to famish, and their store- 78
  houses crammed with grain; make edicts for usury, to   79
  support usurers; repeal daily any wholesome act estab-   80
  lished against the rich, and provide more piercing   81
  statutes daily to chain up and restrain the poor. If the

---

58 *suitors* petitioners   64 *For* as for   65 *dearth* famine   67 *on* go on   70
your impediment the obstruction you raise   73 *transported* carried away   75
helms pilots   78 *suffer* allow   79 *edicts for usury* laws supporting, not out-
lawing, the charging of high interest   81 *piercing* rigorous

wars eat us not up, they will; and there's all the love
they bear us.

MENENIUS
Either you must
86 Confess yourselves wondrous malicious,
Or be accused of folly. I shall tell you
88 A pretty tale. It may be you have heard it,
But, since its serves my purpose, I will venture
90 To stale't a little more.

FIRST CITIZEN   Well, I'll hear it, sir; yet you must not
92 think to fob off our disgrace with a tale. But, an't
please you, deliver.

MENENIUS
94 There was a time when all the body's members
Rebelled against the belly, thus accused it:
That only like a gulf it did remain
I' th' midst o' th' body, idle and unactive,
98 Still cupboarding the viand, never bearing
99 Like labor with the rest, where th' other instruments
100 Did see and hear, devise, instruct, walk, feel,
101 And mutually participate, did minister
102 Unto the appetite and affection common
Of the whole body. The belly answered –

FIRST CITIZEN   Well, sir, what answer made the belly?

MENENIUS
Sir, I shall tell you. With a kind of smile,
106 Which ne'er came from the lungs, but even thus –
For, look you, I may make the belly smile
As well as speak – it tauntingly replied
To th' discontented members, the mutinous parts
110 That envied his receipt; even so most fitly
111 As you malign our senators, for that
112 They are not such as you.

---

86 *wondrous* extraordinarily   88 *pretty* elegant and apt   90 *stale't* make it
stale   92 *fob off* elude; *disgrace* hardship; *an't* if it   94 *members* parts   98
Still always   99 *Like* equal; *instruments* organs   101 *participate* taking part;
minister cater   102 *affection* inclination   106 *lungs* i.e., organ of laughter
110 *his receipt* what he received   111 *for that* because

FIRST CITIZEN   Your belly's answer? What?
 The kingly crownèd head, the vigilant eye,
 The counselor heart, the arm our soldier,
 Our steed the leg, the tongue our trumpeter,
 With other muniments and petty helps   116
 In this our fabric, if that they –
MENENIUS   What then?
 'Fore me, this fellow speaks! What then? what then?   118
FIRST CITIZEN
 Should by the cormorant belly be restrained,   119
 Who is the sink o' th' body –   120
MENENIUS   Well, what then?
FIRST CITIZEN
 The former agents, if they did complain,
 What could the belly answer?
MENENIUS   I will tell you,
 If you'll bestow a small – of what you have little –
 Patience awhile, you'st hear the belly's answer.   124
FIRST CITIZEN
 You're long about it.
MENENIUS   Note me this, good friend;
 Your most grave belly was deliberate,   126
 Not rash like his accusers, and thus answered:
 "True is it, my incorporate friends," quoth he,   128
 "That I receive the general food at first,
 Which you do live upon; and fit it is,   130
 Because I am the storehouse and the shop   131
 Of the whole body. But, if you do remember,
 I send it through the rivers of your blood
 Even to the court, the heart, to th' seat o' th' brain;
 And, through the cranks and offices of man,   135
 The strongest nerves and small inferior veins   136
 From me receive that natural competency   137

---

112 *Your* i.e., the   116 *muniments* furnishings   118 *'Fore me* upon my soul;
speaks is loquacious   119 *cormorant* voracious   124 *you'st* you'll   126 *Your*
this   128 *incorporate* belonging to the body   131 *shop* workshop   135
cranks winding passageways; *offices* workplaces   136 *nerves* sinews   137
competency sufficiency

Whereby they live. And though that all at once" –
You, my good friends! This says the belly. Mark me.
FIRST CITIZEN

140 Ay, sir, well, well.
MENENIUS   "Though all at once cannot
See what I do deliver out to each,

142 Yet I can make my audit up that all
From me do back receive the flour of all,
And leave me but the bran." What say you to't?
FIRST CITIZEN

It was an answer. How apply you this?
MENENIUS

The senators of Rome are this good belly,
And you the mutinous members. For examine

148 Their counsels and their cares, disgest things rightly
149 Touching the weal o' th' common, you shall find
150 No public benefit which you receive
But it proceeds or comes from them to you,
And no way from yourselves. What do you think,
You, the great toe of this assembly?
FIRST CITIZEN

I the great toe! Why the great toe?
MENENIUS

For that, being one o' th' lowest, basest, poorest
Of this most wise rebellion, thou goest foremost.

157 Thou rascal, that art worst in blood to run,
158 Lead'st first to win some vantage.
But make you ready your stiff bats and clubs:

160 Rome and her rats are at the point of battle;
161 The one side must have bale.
          Enter Caius Martius.   Hail, noble Martius!
MARTIUS

162 Thanks. What's the matter, you dissentious rogues,

---

142 *make my audit up* render a full account   148 *disgest* digest   149 *weal o'
th' common* public welfare   157 *rascal* worthless deer; *blood* condition   158
vantage advantage   161 *bale* destruction   162 *dissentious* seditious

That, rubbing the poor itch of your opinion,
Make yourselves scabs?
FIRST CITIZEN   We have ever your good word.
MARTIUS
He that will give good words to thee will flatter
Beneath abhorring. What would you have, you curs,   166
That like nor peace nor war? The one affrights you,   167
The other makes you proud. He that trusts to you,   168
Where he should find you lions, finds you hares;
Where foxes, geese. You are no surer, no,   170
Than is the coal of fire upon the ice,
Or hailstone in the sun. Your virtue is
To make him worthy whose offense subdues him   173
And curse that justice did it. Who deserves greatness   174
Deserves your hate; and your affections are
A sick man's appetite, who desires most that
Which would increase his evil. He that depends
Upon your favors swims with fins of lead
And hews down oaks with rushes. Hang ye! Trust ye?
With every minute you do change a mind,   180
And call him noble that was now your hate,
Him vile that was your garland. What's the matter,   182
That in these several places of the city   183
You cry against the noble Senate, who,
Under the gods, keep you in awe, which else
Would feed on one another? What's their seeking?   186
MENENIUS
For corn at their own rates, whereof they say
The city is well stored.
MARTIUS   Hang 'em! They say?
They'll sit by th' fire and presume to know
What's done i' th' Capitol, who's like to rise,   190

---

166 *beneath abhorring* despicably   167 *nor . . . nor* neither . . . nor; *The one*
i.e., war   168 *The other* i.e., peace   173 *make him worthy* glorify that man;
subdues degrades   174 *that justice* that justice which   182 *garland* hero
183 *several* separate   186 *seeking* petition   190 *like* likely

191 Who thrives and who declines; side factions and give
out
192 Conjectural marriages, making parties strong
193 And feebling such as stand not in their liking
194 Below their cobbled shoes. They say there's grain
enough?
195 Would the nobility lay aside their ruth,
196 And let me use my sword, I'd make a quarry
197 With thousands of these quartered slaves as high
198 As I could pick my lance.

MENENIUS
Nay, these are almost thoroughly persuaded;
200 For though abundantly they lack discretion,
201 Yet are they passing cowardly. But, I beseech you,
What says the other troop?

MARTIUS   They are dissolved. Hang 'em!
203 They said they were anhungry, sighed forth proverbs –
That hunger broke stone walls, that dogs must eat,
That meat was made for mouths, that the gods sent not
206 Corn for the rich men only. With these shreds
They vented their complainings, which being answered
And a petition granted them, a strange one,
209 To break the heart of generosity,
210 And make bold power look pale, they threw their caps
As they would hang them on the horns o' th' moon,
212 Shouting their emulation.

MENENIUS   What is granted them?
MARTIUS
213 Five tribunes to defend their vulgar wisdoms,
Of their own choice. One's Junius Brutus,
215 Sicinius Velutus, and I know not – 'Sdeath!

---

191 *side* take sides with 192 *making* imagining 193 *feebling* making weak
194 *cobbled* mended 195 *ruth* pity 196 *quarry* heap of slaughtered 197
quartered cut in four like criminals 198 *pick* pitch 201 *passing* extremely
203 *anhungry* hungry 206 *shreds* threadbare sayings 209 *generosity* aristocracy 212 *emulation* envy 213 *tribunes* official protectors of the people's
interests; *vulgar* base, popular 215 *'Sdeath* God's death (oath)

The rabble should have first unroofed the city
Ere so prevailed with me; it will in time
Win upon power, and throw forth greater themes   218
For insurrection's arguing.   219
MENENIUS   This is strange.
MARTIUS
  Go, get you home, you fragments!   220
      Enter a Messenger hastily.
MESSENGER
  Where's Caius Martius?
MARTIUS   Here. What's the matter?
MESSENGER
  The news is, sir, the Volsces are in arms.
MARTIUS
  I am glad on't. Then we shall ha' means to vent   223
  Our musty superfluity. See, our best elders.   224
      Enter Sicinius Velutus, Junius Brutus, Cominius, Titus
      Lartius, with other Senators.
FIRST SENATOR
  Martius, 'tis true that you have lately told us: 225
  The Volsces are in arms.
MARTIUS   They have a leader,
  Tullus Aufidius, that will put you to't.   227
  I sin in envying his nobility,
  And were I any thing but what I am,
  I would wish me only he.   230
COMINIUS   You have fought together?
MARTIUS
  Were half to half the world by th' ears and he   231
  Upon my party, I'd revolt, to make   232
  Only my wars with him. He is a lion
  That I am proud to hunt.

---

218 *Win upon power* make further inroads upon authority 219 *For insur-*
rection's arguing to be pursued through rebellion 223 *vent* get rid of 224
musty moldy 225 *that* that which 227 *to't* to the test 230 *together* one
another 231 *by th' ears* at odds 232 *party* side

FIRST SENATOR   Then, worthy Martius,
  Attend upon Cominius to these wars.
COMINIUS
  It is your former promise.
MARTIUS   Sir, it is,
  And I am constant. Titus Lartius, thou
  Shalt see me once more strike at Tullus' face.
239   What, art thou stiff? Stand'st out?
TITUS   No, Caius Martius,
240   I'll lean upon one crutch and fight with t' other,
  Ere stay behind this business.
MENENIUS   O, true-bred!
FIRST SENATOR
  Your company to th' Capitol, where I know
243   Our greatest friends attend us.
TITUS   *[To Cominius]*   Lead you on.
    [To Martius]
  Follow Cominius. We must follow you.
245   Right worthy you priority.
COMINIUS   Noble Martius!
FIRST SENATOR   *[To the Citizens]*
  Hence to your homes, be gone!
MARTIUS   Nay, let them follow.
  The Volsces have much corn. Take these rats thither
248   To gnaw their garners. Worshipful mutineers,
249   Your valor puts well forth. Pray follow.
                              Exeunt. Citizens steal away.
                              Manent Sicinius and Brutus.

SICINIUS
250   Was ever man so proud as is this Martius?
BRUTUS
  He has no equal.
SICINIUS
  When we were chosen tribunes for the people —

---

239 *stiff* reluctant; *Stand'st out* do you keep aloof   **243** *attend* wait   **245**
worthy you priority you are worthy of precedence   **248** *garners* granaries
249 *puts . . . forth* blossoms

BRUTUS
  Marked you his lip and eyes?
SICINIUS   Nay, but his taunts.
BRUTUS
  Being moved, he will not spare to gird the gods.   254
SICINIUS
  Bemock the modest moon.
BRUTUS
  The present wars devour him! He is grown
  Too proud to be so valiant.
SICINIUS   Such a nature,
  Tickled with good success, disdains the shadow
  Which he treads on at noon. But I do wonder
  His insolence can brook to be commanded   260
  Under Cominius.
BRUTUS   Fame, at the which he aims,
  In whom already he's well graced, cannot   262
  Better be held nor more attained than by
  A place below the first; for what miscarries   264
  Shall be the general's fault, though he perform
  To th' utmost of a man, and giddy censure   266
  Will then cry out of Martius, "O, if he
  Had borne the business!"
SICINIUS   Besides, if things go well,
  Opinion, that so sticks on Martius, shall   269
  Of his demerits rob Cominius.   270
BRUTUS   Come.
  Half all Cominius' honors are to Martius,   271
  Though Martius earned them not; and all his faults
  To Martius shall be honors, though indeed
  In aught he merit not.   274
SICINIUS   Let's hence and hear
  How the dispatch is made, and in what fashion,   275

---

254 *spare to gird* desist from taunting   260 *brook* endure   262 *whom* which
264 *miscarries* goes wrong   266 *giddy censure* fickle opinion   269 *so sticks* is
so set   270 *demerits* merits   271 *are to* belong to   274 *aught* anything
275 *dispatch is made* matters are concluded

276   More than his singularity, he goes
        Upon this present action.

BRUTUS   Let's along.   *Exeunt.*

                            *

∾ **I.2** *Enter Tullus Aufidius, with Senators of Corioles.*

FIRST SENATOR
        So, your opinion is, Aufidius,
2   That they of Rome are entered in our counsels
        And know how we proceed.

AUFIDIUS   Is it not yours?
4   What ever have been thought on in this state,
        That could be brought to bodily act ere Rome
6   Had circumvention? 'Tis not four days gone
        Since I heard thence. These are the words. I think
        I have the letter here. Yes, here it is:
9   "They have pressed a power, but it is not known
10   Whether for east or west. The dearth is great,
        The people mutinous; and it is rumored,
        Cominius, Martius your old enemy,
        Who is of Rome worse hated than of you,
        And Titus Lartius, a most valiant Roman,
        These three lead on this preparation
16   Whither 'tis bent. Most likely 'tis for you.
        Consider of it."

FIRST SENATOR   Our army's in the field.
        We never yet made doubt but Rome was ready
        To answer us.

AUFIDIUS   Nor did you think it folly
20   To keep your great pretenses veiled till when
        They needs must show themselves, which in the
            hatching,

---

276 *More than his singularity* personal considerations aside
   I.2 The senate house in Corioles   **2** *entered in* informed of   **4** *What*
what counsels   **6** *circumvention* means of foiling   **9** *pressed a power* raised an
army   **16** *Whither* wherever   **20** *pretenses* designs

It seemed, appeared to Rome. By the discovery   22
  We shall be shortened in our aim, which was   23
  To take in many towns ere almost Rome   24
  Should know we were afoot.
SECOND SENATOR   Noble Aufidius,
  Take your commission; hie you to your bands;
  Let us alone to guard Corioles.
  If they set down before's, for the remove   28
  Bring up your army; but, I think, you'll find
  Th' have not prepared for us.   30
AUFIDIUS   O, doubt not that,
  I speak from certainties. Nay more,
  Some parcels of their power are forth already,   32
  And only hitherward. I leave your honors.
  If we and Caius Martius chance to meet,
  'Tis sworn between us we shall ever strike
  Till one can do no more.
ALL   The gods assist you!
AUFIDIUS
  And keep your honors safe!
FIRST SENATOR   Farewell.
SECOND SENATOR   Farewell.
ALL
  Farewell.   *Exeunt omnes.*

*

∾ **I.3** *Enter Volumnia and Virgilia, mother and wife to
  Martius. They set them down on two low stools and sew.*

VOLUMNIA I pray you, daughter, sing, or express yourself in a more comfortable sort. If my son were my hus- 2
  band, I should freelier rejoice in that absence wherein
  he won honor than in the embracements of his bed
  where he would show most love. When yet he was but

---

22 *appeared* became visible   23 *shortened* reduced   24 *take in* capture   28
for the remove to force their departure   30 *Th'* they   32 *parcels* parts
  I.3 Within the house of Martius   2 *comfortable sort* cheerful manner

tender-bodied and the only son of my womb, when
7 youth with comeliness plucked all gaze his way, when
   for a day of kings' entreaties a mother should not sell
9 him an hour from her beholding, I, considering how
10 honor would become such a person – that it was no
   better than picturelike to hang by th' wall, if renown
   made it not stir – was pleased to let him seek danger
13 where he was like to find fame. To a cruel war I sent
14 him, from whence he returned, his brows bound with
   oak. I tell thee, daughter, I sprang not more in joy at
   first hearing he was a man-child than now in first seeing he had proved himself a man.

VIRGILIA   But had he died in the business, madam, how
   then?

20 VOLUMNIA   Then his good report should have been my
21 son; I therein would have found issue. Hear me profess
   sincerely: had I a dozen sons, each in my love alike, and
   none less dear than thine and my good Martius, I had
   rather had eleven die nobly for their country than one
25 voluptuously surfeit out of action.

       Enter a Gentlewoman.

GENTLEWOMAN
   Madam, the Lady Valeria is come to visit you.

VIRGILIA
27 Beseech you, give me leave to retire myself.

VOLUMNIA
   Indeed, you shall not.
   Methinks I hear hither your husband's drum;
30 See him pluck Aufidius down by th' hair;
   As children from a bear, the Volsces shunning him.
   Methinks I see him stamp thus, and call thus:
33 "Come on, you cowards! You were got in fear,
   Though you were born in Rome." His bloody brow

---

7 *comeliness* beauty; *plucked all gaze* attracted the attention of all   9 *from her beholding* out of her sight   10 *person* body   13 *like* likely   14–15 *bound with oak* crowned for saving a Roman citizen in battle   21 *issue* progeny   25 *surfeit* overindulge himself   27 *Beseech* I beseech   33 *got* begotten

With his mailed hand then wiping, forth he goes,   35
Like to a harvestman that's tasked to mow   36
Or all or lose his hire.

VIRGILIA
His bloody brow? O Jupiter, no blood!   38

VOLUMNIA
Away, you fool! It more becomes a man
Than gilt his trophy. The breasts of Hecuba,   40
When she did suckle Hector, looked not lovelier   41
Than Hector's forehead when it spit forth blood
At Grecian sword, contemning. Tell Valeria,   43
We are fit to bid her welcome.   *Exit Gentlewoman.*

VIRGILIA
Heavens bless my lord from fell Aufidius!   45

VOLUMNIA
He'll beat Aufidius' head below his knee
And tread upon his neck.
     Enter Valeria, with an Usher and a Gentlewoman.

VALERIA   My ladies both, good day to you.

VOLUMNIA   Sweet madam.

VIRGILIA   I am glad to see your ladyship.   50

VALERIA   How do you both? You are manifest house-   51
keepers. What are you sewing here? A fine spot, in good 52
faith. How does your little son?

VIRGILIA   I thank your ladyship; well, good madam.

VOLUMNIA   He had rather see the swords and hear a
drum than look upon his schoolmaster.

VALERIA   O' my word, the father's son! I'll swear 'tis a very 57
pretty boy. O' my troth, I looked upon him o' Wednes-
day half an hour together. 'Has such a confirmed coun- 59
tenance! I saw him run after a gilded butterfly, and   60
when he caught it, he let it go again, and after it again,

---

35 *mailed* armored   **36–37** *Like . . . hire* like a laborer hired to mow a whole crop or not be paid for any of it   **38** *Jupiter* king of the gods and patron of Rome   **40** *gilt his trophy* gilding becomes his monument; *Hecuba* queen of Troy   **41** *Hector* Trojan champion   **43** *contemning* despising   **45** *bless* protect; *fell* deadly   **51–52** *housekeepers* housewives, stay-at-homes   **52** *spot* embroidered figure   **57** *O'* on   **59** *confirmed* resolute

and over and over he comes, and up again, catched it
63   again. Or whether his fall enraged him, or how 'twas, he
did so set his teeth and tear it! Oh, I warrant, how he
65   mammocked it!

66 VOLUMNIA   One on's father's moods.

VALERIA   Indeed, la, 'tis a noble child.

68 VIRGILIA   A crack, madam.

VALERIA   Come, lay aside your stitchery. I must have you
70   play the idle housewife with me this afternoon.

VIRGILIA   No, good madam, I will not out of doors.

VALERIA   Not out of doors?

VOLUMNIA   She shall, she shall.

74 VIRGILIA   Indeed, no, by your patience. I'll not over the
threshold till my lord return from the wars.

VALERIA   Fie, you confine yourself most unreasonably.
77   Come, you must go visit the good lady that lies in.

VIRGILIA   I will wish her speedy strength and visit her
with my prayers, but I cannot go thither.

80 VOLUMNIA   Why, I pray you?

81 VIRGILIA   'Tis not to save labor, nor that I want love.

82 VALERIA   You would be another Penelope; yet they say all
83   the yarn she spun in Ulysses' absence did but fill Ithaca
full of moths. Come, I would your cambric were
85   sensible as your finger, that you might leave pricking it
for pity. Come, you shall go with us.

VIRGILIA   No, good madam, pardon me; indeed I will
not forth.

VALERIA   In truth, la, go with me, and I'll tell you excel-
90   lent news of your husband.

VIRGILIA   O, good madam, there can be none yet.

92 VALERIA   Verily, I do not jest with you. There came news
from him last night.

VIRGILIA   Indeed, madam?

---

63 *Or whether* whether; *how* however 65 *mammocked* tore to pieces 66 *on's* of his 68 *crack* imp 74 *by your patience* if you please 77 *lies in* expects a child 81 *want* am lacking in 82 *Penelope* faithful wife of Ulysses, who put off her suitors by weaving 83 *Ithaca* Ulysses' kingdom in Homer's *Odyssey* 85 *sensible* capable of sensation; *leave* stop 92 *Verily* truly

VALERIA   In earnest, it's true. I heard a senator speak it.
Thus it is: the Volsces have an army forth, against
whom Cominius the general is gone with one part of
our Roman power. Your lord and Titus Lartius are set
down before their city Corioles. They nothing doubt
prevailing and to make it brief wars. This is true, on   100
mine honor; and so, I pray, go with us.

VIRGILIA   Give me excuse, good madam. I will obey you   102
in everything hereafter.

VOLUMNIA   Let her alone, lady. As she is now, she will
but disease our better mirth.   105

VALERIA   In troth, I think she would. Fare you well, then.
Come, good sweet lady. Prithee, Virgilia, turn thy
solemness out o' door and go along with us.

VIRGILIA   No, at a word, madam. Indeed, I must not. I
wish you much mirth.   *110*

VALERIA   Well, then, farewell.   *Exeunt.*

※

∿ **I.4** *Enter Martius, Titus Lartius, with [a trumpeter],
Drum and Colors, with Captains and Soldiers, as
before the city Corioles. To them a Messenger.*

MARTIUS
Yonder comes news. A wager they have met.

LARTIUS
My horse to yours, no.

MARTIUS   'Tis done.

LARTIUS   Agreed.

MARTIUS
Say, has our general met the enemy?

MESSENGER
They lie in view, but have not spoke as yet.   4

---

100 *prevailing* winning   **102** *Give me excuse* excuse me   **105** *disease* make
uneasy; *better mirth* enjoyment that will be greater without her
   I.4 Before the gates of Corioles   **4** *spoke* encountered

LARTIUS
    So, the good horse is mine.
MARTIUS   I'll buy him of you.
LARTIUS
    No, I'll nor sell nor give him. Lend you him I will
    For half a hundred years. *[To trumpeter]* Summon the
      town.
MARTIUS
    How far off lie these armies?
MESSENGER   Within this mile and half.
MARTIUS
9   Then shall we hear their 'larum, and they ours.
10   Now, Mars, I prithee, make us quick in work,
11   That we with smoking swords may march from hence,
12   To help our fielded friends! Come, blow thy blast.
          They sound a parley.
          Enter two Senators, with others, on the walls of
          Corioles.
    Tullus Aufidius, is he within your walls?
FIRST SENATOR
    No, nor a man that fears you less than he:
15   That's lesser than a little.
          Drum afar off.   Hark! our drums
    Are bringing forth our youth. We'll break our walls
17   Rather than they shall pound us up. Our gates,
    Which yet seem shut, we have but pinned with rushes;
    They'll open of themselves.
          Alarum afar off.   Hark you, far off!
20   There is Aufidius. List what work he makes
21   Amongst your cloven army.
MARTIUS   O, they are at it!
LARTIUS
22   Their noise be our instruction. Ladders, ho!

---

9 *'larum* call to arms   11 *smoking* hot with slaughter   12 *fielded* in the battlefield   15 *lesser than a little* next to nothing   17 *pound* pen   20 *list* listen
21 *cloven* split   22 *our instruction* a lesson to us

Enter the army of the Volsces.

MARTIUS

They fear us not, but issue forth their city.   23
Now put your shields before your hearts, and fight
With hearts more proof than shields. Advance, brave   25
  Titus.
They do disdain us much beyond our thoughts,   26
Which makes me sweat with wrath. Come on, my
  fellows.
He that retires, I'll take him for a Volsce,
And he shall feel mine edge.   29
  Alarum. The Romans are beat back to their trenches.
  Enter Martius, cursing.

MARTIUS

All the contagion of the south light on you,   30
You shames of Rome! you herd of – Boils and plagues
Plaster you o'er, that you may be abhorred   32
Farther than seen, and one infect another
Against the wind a mile! You souls of geese,   34
That bear the shapes of men, how have you run
From slaves that apes would beat! Pluto and hell!
All hurt behind! backs red, and faces pale
With flight and agued fear! Mend and charge home,   38
Or, by the fires of heaven, I'll leave the foe
And make my wars on you! Look to't. Come on!   40
If you'll stand fast, we'll beat them to their wives,
As they us to our trenches. Follow me!
  Another alarum and Martius follows them to gates
  and is shut in.
So, now the gates are ope. Now prove good seconds.   43
'Tis for the followers fortune widens them,   44
Not for the fliers. Mark me, and do the like.   45

---

23 *issue forth* march out of **25** *proof* impenetrable **26** *beyond our thoughts* more than we expected **29** *edge* sword **30** *contagion* infection **32–33** *abhorred . . . seen* smell disgusting even before you're seen **34** *against . . . a mile* against the wind, even a mile away **38** *agued* trembling; *home* to the utmost **43** *ope* open; *seconds* supporters **44** *followers* pursuers **45** *fliers* pursued

Enter the gates.

FIRST SOLDIER
Foolhardiness, not I.

SECOND SOLDIER   Nor I.

FIRST SOLDIER
47   See, they have shut him in.
Alarum continues.

ALL   To th' pot, I warrant him.
Enter Titus Lartius.

LARTIUS
What is become of Martius?

ALL   Slain, sir, doubtless.

FIRST SOLDIER
Following the fliers at the very heels,
50   With them he enters, who upon the sudden
Clapped to their gates; he is himself alone,
To answer all the city.

LARTIUS   O noble fellow!
53   Who sensibly outdares his senseless sword,
54   And, when it bows, stand'st up. Thou art lost, Martius.
55   A carbuncle entire, as big as thou art,
Were not so rich a jewel. Thou wast a soldier
57   Even to Cato's wish, not fierce and terrible
Only in strokes; but with thy grim looks and
The thunderlike percussion of thy sounds,
60   Thou mad'st thine enemies shake, as if the world
61   Were feverous and did tremble.
Enter Martius, bleeding, assaulted by the Enemy.

FIRST SOLDIER   Look, sir.

LARTIUS   O, 'tis, Martius!
62   Let's fetch him off, or make remain alike.
They fight, and all enter the City.

*

---

47 *To th' pot* i.e., he's as good as cooked   53 *sensibly* feelingly; *senseless* insensate   54 *bows* bends   55 *carbuncle entire* flawless gemstone   57 *Cato* the Censor, severe Roman moralist   61 *feverous* feverish   62 *make remain alike* stay there similarly

∾ **I.5** *Enter certain Romans, with spoils.*

FIRST ROMAN   This will I carry to Rome.
SECOND ROMAN   And I this.
THIRD ROMAN   A murrain on't! I took this for silver.   3
    Alarum continues still afar off.
    Enter Martius and Titus Lartius, with a Trumpet.
MARTIUS
  See here these movers that do prize their hours   4
  At a cracked drachma! Cushions, leaden spoons,   5
  Irons of a doit, doublets that hangmen would   6
  Bury with those that wore them, these base slaves,
  Ere yet the fight be done, pack up. Down with them!
  And hark, what noise the general makes! To him!
  There is the man of my soul's hate, Aufidius,   10
  Piercing our Romans. Then, valiant Titus, take
  Convenient numbers to make good the city;   12
  Whilst I, with those that have the spirit, will haste
  To help Cominius.
LARTIUS   Worthy sir, thou bleed'st.
  Thy exercise hath been too violent
  For a second course of fight.   16
MARTIUS   Sir, praise me not.
  My work hath yet not warmed me. Fare you well.
  The blood I drop is rather physical   18
  Than dangerous to me. To Aufidius thus
  I will appear and fight.   20
LARTIUS   Now the fair goddess Fortune
  Fall deep in love with thee, and her great charms   21
  Misguide thy opposers' swords! Bold gentleman,
  Prosperity be thy page!

I.5 A street in Corioles   3 *murrain* cattle plague   s.d. *Trumpet* trumpeter
4 *movers* active men; *prize their hours* value their time   5 *drachma* Greek
coin   6 *of a doit* worth the smallest sum; *doublets* close-fitting garments;
hangmen (whose perquisites included the clothes of the hanged)   12 *make
good* secure   16 *course* round; *praise* appraise   18 *physical* curative   21
charms magic spells

MARTIUS   Thy friend no less
24   Than those she placeth highest. So, farewell.
LARTIUS
     Thou worthiest Martius!   [Exit Martius.]
     Go sound thy trumpet in the marketplace.
27   Call thither all the officers o' th' town,
     Where they shall know our mind. Away!   Exeunt.

                         *

   ～ I.6 *Enter Cominius, as it were in retire, with Soldiers.*

COMINIUS
     Breathe you, my friends. Well fought! We are come off
     Like Romans, neither foolish in our stands
3   Nor cowardly in retire. Believe me, sirs,
     We shall be charged again. Whiles we have struck,
5   By interims and conveying gusts we have heard
     The charges of our friends. The Roman gods
7   Lead their successes as we wish our own,
8   That both our powers, with smiling fronts encount'ring,
     May give you thankful sacrifice.
             Enter a Messenger.   Thy news?
MESSENGER
10   The citizens of Corioles have issued,
     And given to Lartius and to Martius battle.
     I saw our party to their trenches driven,
     And then I came away.
COMINIUS   Though thou speakest truth,
     Methinks thou speak'st not well. How long is't since?
MESSENGER
     Above an hour, my lord.
COMINIUS
16   'Tis not a mile; briefly we heard their drums.

---

24 *those* friend to those   27 *officers* officeholders
   I.6 An open place near the Roman camp   3 *retire* withdrawal   5 *by in-*
terims at intervals; *conveying* carrying the noise of battle   7 *successes* fortunes
8 *fronts* faces   10 *issued* sallied forth   16 *briefly* a short while ago

How couldst thou in a mile confound an hour, 17
And bring thy news so late?
MESSENGER   Spies of the Volsces
Held me in chase, that I was forced to wheel 19
Three or four miles about; else had I, sir, 20
Half an hour since brought my report.
COMINIUS   Who's yonder,
That does appear as he were flayed? O gods! 22
He has the stamp of Martius, and I have 23
Beforetime seen him thus. 24
 Enter Martius.
MARTIUS   Come I too late?
COMINIUS
The shepherd knows not thunder from a tabor 25
More than I know the sound of Martius' tongue
From every meaner man. 27
MARTIUS   Come I too late?
COMINIUS
Ay, if you come not in the blood of others,
But mantled in your own. 29
MARTIUS   O, let me clip ye
In arms as sound as when I wooed, in heart 30
As merry as when our nuptial day was done,
And tapers burned to bedward! 32
COMINIUS   Flower of warriors!
How is't with Titus Lartius?
MARTIUS
As with a man busied about decrees:
Condemning some to death, and some to exile;
Ransoming him or pitying, threatening th' other; 36
Holding Corioles in the name of Rome,
Even like a fawning greyhound in the leash,
To let him slip at will. 39

---

17 *confound* waste 19 *that* so that 22 *flayed* skinned 23 *stamp* imprint
24 *Beforetime* in former time 25 *tabor* small drum 27 *meaner* lesser 29
clip embrace 32 *tapers burned to bedward* candles indicated bedtime 36
Ransoming releasing 39 *let him slip* unleash him

COMINIUS   Where is that slave
40   Which told me they had beat you to your trenches?
Where is he? Call him hither.
MARTIUS   Let him alone.
He did inform the truth. But for our gentlemen,
43   The common file – a plague! tribunes for them! –
44   The mouse ne'er shunned the cat as they did budge
From rascals worse than they.
COMINIUS   But how prevailed you?
MARTIUS
Will the time serve to tell? I do not think.
Where is the enemy? Are you lords o' th' field?
If not, why cease you till you are so?
COMINIUS   Martius,
We have at disadvantage fought and did
50   Retire to win our purpose.
MARTIUS
51   How lies their battle? Know you on which side
They have placed their men of trust?
COMINIUS   As I guess, Martius,
53   Their bands i' th' vaward are the Antiates,
Of their best trust; o'er them Aufidius,
Their very heart of hope.
MARTIUS   I do beseech you
By all the battles wherein we have fought,
By th' blood we have shed together,
By the vows we have made
59   To endure friends, that you directly set me
60   Against Aufidius and his Antiates,
61   And that you not delay the present, but,
Filling the air with swords advanced and darts,
63   We prove this very hour.

---

43 *common file* rank and file   44 *budge* retreat   51 *How lies their battle* how are their forces drawn up   53 *vaward* vanguard; *Antiates* those from Antium   59 *endure* remain   61 *delay the present* delay now   63 *prove* put things to the test

COMINIUS   Though I could wish
   You were conducted to a gentle bath
   And balms applied to you, yet dare I never
   Deny your asking. Take your choice of those
   That best can aid your action.

MARTIUS   Those are they
   That most are willing. If any such be here –
   As it were sin to doubt – that love this painting
   Wherein you see me smeared; if any fear   70
   Lesser his person than an ill report;
   If any think brave death outweighs bad life,
   And that his country 's dearer than himself;
   Let him alone, or so many so minded,
   Wave thus, to express his disposition,
   And follow Martius.
      They all shout and wave their swords, take him up in
      their arms, and cast up their caps.
   O, me alone! Make you a sword of me?
   If these shows be not outward, which of you   78
   But is four Volsces? None of you but is
   Able to bear against the great Aufidius   80
   A shield as hard as his. A certain number,
   Though thanks to all, must I select. The rest
   Shall bear the business in some other fight,
   As cause will be obeyed. Please you to march;   84
   And four shall quickly draw out my command,   85
   Which men are best inclined.

COMINIUS   March on, my fellows.
   Make good this ostentation, and you shall   87
   Divide in all with us.   *Exeunt.*   88

                     *

70–71 *fear Lesser* fear less for   78 *shows* gestures   84 *cause will be obeyed* circumstances require   85 *draw out* select from   87 *Make . . . ostentation* live up to these appearances   88 *divide* share

❧ **I.7** *Titus Lartius, having set a guard upon Corioles,*
going with Drum and Trumpet toward Cominius and
Caius Martius, enters with a Lieutenant, other
Soldiers, and a Scout.

LARTIUS

1⠀⠀So, let the ports be guarded. Keep your duties,
⠀⠀⠀As I have set them down. If I do send, dispatch
3⠀⠀Those centuries to our aid; the rest will serve
⠀⠀⠀For a short holding. If we lose the field,
5⠀⠀We cannot keep the town.

LIEUTENANT⠀⠀⠀⠀⠀⠀⠀⠀⠀⠀⠀⠀⠀⠀Fear not our care, sir.

LARTIUS

⠀⠀⠀Hence, and shut your gates upon's.
7⠀⠀Our guider, come; to th' Roman camp conduct us.

⠀⠀⠀⠀⠀⠀⠀⠀⠀⠀⠀⠀⠀⠀⠀⠀⠀⠀⠀⠀⠀⠀⠀⠀*Exeunt.*

*

❧ **I.8** *Alarum, as in battle. Enter Martius and Aufidius*
at several doors.

MARTIUS

⠀⠀⠀I'll fight with none but thee, for I do hate thee
⠀⠀⠀Worse than a promise breaker.

AUFIDIUS⠀⠀⠀⠀⠀⠀⠀⠀⠀⠀⠀⠀⠀⠀⠀We hate alike.

3⠀⠀Not Afric owns a serpent I abhor
4⠀⠀More than thy fame and envy. Fix thy foot.

MARTIUS

⠀⠀⠀Let the first budger die the other's slave,
⠀⠀⠀And the gods doom him after!

AUFIDIUS⠀⠀⠀⠀⠀⠀⠀⠀⠀⠀⠀⠀⠀⠀⠀If I fly, Martius,

7⠀⠀Hollo me like a hare.

I.7 *Before the gates of Corioles* **1** *ports* gates **3** *centuries* companies of a
hundred **3–4** *serve . . . holding* i.e., will hold their ground for the moment
5 *Fear not* do not doubt **7** *guider* guide

⠀⠀**I.8** An open place near the Roman camp **s.d.** *at several doors* from different entrances **3** *Afric* Africa **4** *fame and envy* enviable fame **7** *Hollo*
hunt down

MARTIUS   Within these three hours, Tullus,
  Alone I fought in your Corioles walls,
  And made what work I pleased. 'Tis not my blood
  Wherein thou seest me masked. For thy revenge   10
  Wrench up thy power to th' highest.
AUFIDIUS   Wert thou the Hector
  That was the whip of your bragged progeny,   12
  Thou shouldst not scape me here.   13
    *Here they fight, and certain Volsces come in the aid of
    Aufidius. Martius fights till they be driven in
    breathless.*
  Officious and not valiant, you have shamed me   14
  In your condemnèd seconds.   *[Exeunt.]*   15

                      *

∾ **I.9** *Alarum. A retreat is sounded. Flourish. Enter, at
  one door, Cominius with the Romans; at another door,
  Martius with his arm in a scarf.*

COMINIUS
  If I should tell thee o'er this thy day's work,   1
  Thou't not believe thy deeds. But I'll report it   2
  Where senators shall mingle tears with smiles;
  Where great patricians shall attend and shrug,
  I' th' end admire; where ladies shall be frighted,   5
  And, gladly quaked, hear more; where the dull tribunes, 6
  That with the fusty plebeians hate thine honors,   7
  Shall say against their hearts, "We thank the gods
  Our Rome hath such a soldier."
  Yet camest thou to a morsel of this feast,   10
  Having fully dined before.
    *Enter Titus [Lartius], with his Power, from the
    pursuit.*

---

12 *whip* champion; *bragged progeny* boasted progenitors 13 *scape* escape
14 *Officious* meddling 15 *condemnèd seconds* shameful support
  I.9 1 *tell thee o'er* relate to you 2 *Thou't* thou wouldst 5 *admire* marvel 6 *gladly quaked* pleasingly terrified 7 *fusty* moldy; *plebeians* people of
the lowest Roman class

LARTIUS   O general,
12 Here is the steed, we the caparison.
    Hadst thou beheld –
MARTIUS   Pray now, no more. My mother,
14 Who has a charter to extol her blood,
    When she does praise me grieves me.
    I have done as you have done – that's what I can;
    Induced as you have been – that's for my country.
18 He that has but effected his good will
    Hath overta'en mine act.
19 COMINIUS   You shall not be
20 The grave of your deserving. Rome must know
    The value of her own. 'Twere a concealment
22 Worse than a theft, no less than a traducement,
    To hide your doings and to silence that
24 Which, to the spire and top of praises vouched,
25 Would seem but modest. Therefore, I beseech you –
26 In sign of what you are, not to reward
    What you have done – before our army hear me.
MARTIUS
    I have some wounds upon me, and they smart
    To hear themselves remembered.
COMINIUS   Should they not,
30 Well might they fester 'gainst ingratitude
31 And tent themselves with death. Of all the horses,
32 Whereof we have ta'en good and good store, of all
    The treasure in this field achieved and city,
    We render you the tenth, to be ta'en forth
    Before the common distribution at
36 Your only choice.
MARTIUS   I thank you, general,
    But cannot make my heart consent to take
    A bribe to pay my sword. I do refuse it,

---

12 *caparison* trappings   14 *charter* privilege   18 *effected his good will* accom-
plished his intention   19–20 *You . . . deserving* you shall not bury your
merit   22 *traducement* slander   24 *vouched* attested   25 *modest* moderate
26 *sign* token   30 *'gainst* on account of   31 *tent* cure by probing   32 *good
and good store* good in quality and quantity   36 *only* sole

And stand upon my common part with those
That have beheld the doing.   40
> *A long flourish. They all cry, "Martius! Martius!", cast*
> *up their caps and lances. Cominius and Lartius stand*
> *bare.*

MARTIUS
May these same instruments which you profane
Never sound more! When drums and trumpets shall
I' th' field prove flatterers, let courts and cities be
Made all of false-faced soothing!   44
When steel grows soft as the parasite's silk,
Let him be made a coverture for th' wars.   46
No more, I say! For that I have not washed
My nose that bled, or foiled some debile wretch,   48
Which without note here's many else have done,   49
You shout me forth in acclamations hyperbolical,   50
As if I loved my little should be dieted   51
In praises sauced with lies.
COMINIUS   Too modest are you,
More cruel to your good report than grateful
To us that give you truly. By your patience,   54
If 'gainst yourself you be incensed, we'll put you,
Like one that means his proper harm, in manacles,   56
Then reason safely with you. Therefore be it known,
As to us, to all the world, that Caius Martius
Wears this war's garland; in token of the which,   59
My noble steed, known to the camp, I give him,   60
With all his trim belonging; and from this time,   61
For what he did before Corioles, call him,
With all th' applause and clamor of the host,
Caius Martius Coriolanus. Bear
Th' addition nobly ever!   65
> *Flourish. Trumpets sound, and drums.*

---

44 *false-faced soothing* hypocritical flattery 46 *him* i.e., the silk; *coverture* covering 48 *foiled* have defeated; *debile* weak 49 *without note* unnoticed 51 *little* small share; *dieted* fed 54 *give* represent 56 *means* intends; *proper* own 59 *Wears . . . garland* is this war's hero 61 *trim belonging* appertaining equipment 65 *addition* title

ALL
    Caius Martius Coriolanus!
CORIOLANUS
    I will go wash;
68   And when my face is fair, you shall perceive
    Whether I blush or no. Howbeit, I thank you.
70   I mean to stride your steed, and at all times
71   To undercrest your good addition
72   To th' fairness of my power.
COMINIUS   So, to our tent,
    Where, ere we do repose us, we will write
    To Rome of our success. You, Titus Lartius,
    Must to Corioles back. Send us to Rome
76   The best, with whom we may articulate,
    For their own good and ours.
LARTIUS   I shall, my lord.
CORIOLANUS
    The gods begin to mock me. I, that now
    Refused most princely gifts, am bound to beg
80   Of my lord general.
COMINIUS   Take't, 'tis yours. What is't?
CORIOLANUS
81   I sometime lay here in Corioles
82   At a poor man's house; he used me kindly.
83   He cried to me; I saw him prisoner;
    But then Aufidius was within my view,
    And wrath o'erwhelmed my pity. I request you
    To give my poor host freedom.
COMINIUS   O, well begged!
    Were he the butcher of my son, he should
88   Be free as is the wind. Deliver him, Titus.
LARTIUS
    Martius, his name?

---

68 *fair* clean   71 *undercrest* adopt and justify (heraldic)   72 *To . . . power* to the best of my ability   76 *articulate* come to terms   81 *sometime lay* once lodged   82 *used* treated   83 *cried* cried out   88 *deliver* release

CORIOLANUS   By Jupiter, forgot!
  I am weary; yea, my memory is tired.   90
  Have we no wine here?
COMINIUS   Go we to our tent.
  The blood upon your visage dries; 'tis time
  It should be looked to. Come.   *Exeunt.*

                          ✳

❧ **I.10** *A flourish. Cornets. Enter Tullus Aufidius,*
      bloody, with two or three Soldiers.

AUFIDIUS
  The town is ta'en.
FIRST SOLDIER
    'Twill be delivered back on good condition.   2
AUFIDIUS
  Condition?
  I would I were a Roman; for I cannot,
  Being a Volsce, be that I am. Condition?   5
  What good condition can a treaty find
  I' th' part that is at mercy? Five times, Martius,   7
  I have fought with thee; so often hast thou beat me,
  And wouldst do so, I think, should we encounter
  As often as we eat. By th' elements,   10
  If e'er again I meet him beard to beard,
  He's mine or I am his. Mine emulation   12
  Hath not that honor in't it had; for where
  I thought to crush him in an equal force,
  True sword to sword, I'll potch at him some way;   15
  Or wrath or craft may get him.   16
FIRST SOLDIER   He's the devil.
AUFIDIUS
  Bolder, though not so subtle. My valor's poisoned

————————————

I.10 *The camp of the Volsces* **2** *good condition* favorable terms **5** *be that I
am* be what I really am **7** *I' th' part* for the side; *at mercy* in the victor's
power **12** *emulation* rivalry **15** *potch* make a stab **16** *or . . . or* either . . .
or

With only suffering stain by him; for him
19   Shall fly out of itself. Nor sleep nor sanctuary,
20   Being naked, sick, nor fane nor capitol,
The prayers of priests nor times of sacrifice,
22   Embargements all of fury, shall lift up
Their rotten privilege and custom 'gainst
My hate to Martius. Where I find him, were it
25   At home, upon my brother's guard, even there,
26   Against the hospitable canon, would I
Wash my fierce hand in's heart. Go you to th' city.
Learn how 'tis held, and what they are that must
Be hostages for Rome.

FIRST SOLDIER   Will not you go?

AUFIDIUS
30   I am attended at the cypress grove: I pray you –
'Tis south the city mills – bring me word thither
How the world goes, that to the pace of it
I may spur on my journey.

FIRST SOLDIER   I shall, sir.   *[Exeunt.]*

*

∾ **II.1** *Enter Menenius, with the two Tribunes of the
People, Sicinius and Brutus.*

1 MENENIUS   The augurer tells me we shall have news
tonight.

BRUTUS   Good or bad?

MENENIUS   Not according to the prayer of the people,
for they love not Martius.

SICINIUS   Nature teaches beasts to know their friends.

MENENIUS   Pray you, who does the wolf love?

SICINIUS   The lamb.

MENENIUS   Ay, to devour him, as the hungry plebeians
10 would the noble Martius.

---

19 *Shall . . . itself* shall deviate from its nature   20 *fane* shrine   22 *Embargements* restraints   25 *upon* under   26 *hospitable canon* law of hospitality   30 *attended* awaited
II.1 A public place in Rome   1 *augurer* soothsayer

BRUTUS   He's a lamb indeed, that baas like a bear.

MENENIUS   He's a bear indeed, that lives like a lamb. You
two are old men: tell me one thing that I shall ask you.

BOTH   Well, sir.

MENENIUS   In what enormity is Martius poor in, that   15
you two have not in abundance?

BRUTUS   He's poor in no one fault, but stored with all.

SICINIUS   Especially in pride.

BRUTUS   And topping all others in boasting.

MENENIUS   This is strange now. Do you two know how   20
you are censured here in the city, I mean of us o' th'   21
right-hand file? Do you?   22

BOTH   Why, how are we censured?

MENENIUS   Because you talk of pride now – will you not
be angry?

BOTH   Well, well, sir, well.

MENENIUS   Why, 'tis no great matter, for a very little   27
thief of occasion will rob you of a great deal of patience.
Give your dispositions the reins and be angry at your
pleasures – at the least, if you take it as a pleasure to   30
you in being so. You blame Martius for being proud?

BRUTUS   We do it not alone, sir.

MENENIUS   I know you can do very little alone, for your
helps are many, or else your actions would grow
wondrous single. Your abilities are too infantlike for   35
doing much alone. You talk of pride: O that you could
turn your eyes toward the napes of your necks, and
make but an interior survey of your good selves! O that
you could!

BRUTUS   What then, sir?   40

MENENIUS   Why, then you should discover a brace of un-   41
meriting, proud, violent, testy magistrates, alias fools,
as any in Rome.

---

15 *enormity* vice; *poor in* degraded by   **21** *censured* judged   **22** *right-hand
file* ruling class   **27–28** *a very . . . patience* you get very impatient upon the
slightest pretext   **35** *wondrous single* extraordinarily feeble   **41** *brace* pair

44 SICINIUS   Menenius, you are known well enough too.

45 MENENIUS   I am known to be a humorous patrician, and
      one that loves a cup of hot wine with not a drop of allay-
47   ing Tiber in't; said to be something imperfect in fa-
      voring the first complaint; hasty and tinderlike upon
49   too trivial motion; one that converses more with the
50   buttock of the night than with the forehead of the
51   morning. What I think, I utter, and spend my malice in
52   my breath. Meeting two such wealsmen as you are, I
53   cannot call you Lycurguses. If the drink you give me
      touch my palate adversely, I make a crooked face at it. I
      cannot say your worships have delivered the matter
56   well, when I find the ass in compound with the major
      part of your syllables. And though I must be content to
58   bear with those that say you are reverend grave men,
      yet they lie deadly that tell you you have good faces. If
60   you see this in the map of my microcosm, follows it
      that I am known well enough too? What harm can
62   your bisson conspectuities glean out of this character, if
      I be known well enough too?

   BRUTUS   Come, sir, come, we know you well enough.

   MENENIUS   You know neither me, yourselves, nor any-
66   thing. You are ambitious for poor knaves' caps and legs.
      You wear out a good wholesome forenoon in hearing a
68   cause between an orange wife and a forset seller, and
69   then rejourn the controversy of threepence to a second
70   day of audience. When you are hearing a matter be-
      tween party and party, if you chance to be pinched with
72   the colic, you make faces like mummers; set up the

------

44 *known well enough* i.e., notorious   45 *humorous* whimsical   45–47 *allay-
ing Tiber* diluting river water   47–48 *imperfect . . . complaint* partial toward
the first speaker (complainant)   49 *motion* motive   49–51 *one . . . morning*
more used to staying up late than rising early   51 *spend my malice* expend
my ill will   52 *wealsmen* statesmen   53 *Lycurges* Spartan lawgiver   56 *ass in
compound* i.e., "ass" is included in "whereas"   58 *reverend* respected   60
map face; *microcosm* body   62 *bisson conspectuities* bleared eyesights;   *character* character sketch   66 *caps* doffing of hats; *legs* bows   68 *orange wife*
street vendor; *forset* wine tap   69 *rejourn* adjourn   70 *audience* hearing   72
mummers masqueraders   72–73 *set . . . against* declare war on

bloody flag against all patience, and, in roaring for a
chamber pot, dismiss the controversy bleeding, the 74
more entangled by your hearing. All the peace you
make in their cause is calling both the parties knaves.
You are a pair of strange ones.

BRUTUS Come, come, you are well understood to be a 78
perfecter giber for the table than a necessary bencher in
the Capitol. 80

MENENIUS Our very priests must become mockers, if
they shall encounter such ridiculous subjects as you are.
When you speak best unto the purpose, it is not worth
the wagging of your beards, and your beards deserve
not so honorable a grave as to stuff a botcher's cushion 85
or to be entombed in an ass's packsaddle. Yet you must
be saying Martius is proud; who, in a cheap estimation, 87
is worth all your predecessors since Deucalion, though 88
peradventure some of the best of 'em were hereditary 89
hangmen. Good-e'en to your worships. More of your 90
conversation would infect my brain, being the herds- 91
men of the beastly plebeians. I will be bold to take my
leave of you.

Brutus and Sicinius aside.
Enter Volumnia, Virgilia, and Valeria.

How now, my as fair as noble ladies – and the moon,
were she earthly, no nobler – whither do you follow
your eyes so fast?

VOLUMNIA Honorable Menenius, my boy Martius approaches. For the love of Juno, let's go. 98

MENENIUS Ha? Martius coming home?

VOLUMNIA Ay, worthy Menenius, and with most pros- *100*
perous approbation. 101

---

74 *bleeding* unhealed   78–79 *a perfecter . . . Capitol* rather a dinner-table wit
than a serious legislator   85 *botcher* clothes mender   87 *cheap estimation*
low estimate   88 *Deucalion* survivor of the Flood   89 *peradventure* perhaps
90 *Good-e'en* good evening   91 *being* since you are   98 *Juno* chief Roman
goddess, sister and wife of Jupiter   101 *approbation* approval

102 MENENIUS   Take my cap, Jupiter, and I thank thee. Hoo,
   Martius coming home!

TWO LADIES   Nay, 'tis true.

VOLUMNIA   Look, here's a letter from him. The state
   hath another, his wife another; and, I think, there's one
   at home for you.

MENENIUS   I will make my very house reel tonight. A letter for me?

110 VIRGILIA   Yes, certain, there's a letter for you; I saw't.

MENENIUS   A letter for me! It gives me an estate of seven
112   years' health, in which time I will make a lip at the
113   physician. The most sovereign prescription in Galen is
114   but empiricutic and, to this preservative, of no better
115   report than a horse drench. Is he not wounded? He was
   wont to come home wounded.

VIRGILIA   O, no, no, no.

VOLUMNIA   O, he is wounded; I thank the gods for't.

119 MENENIUS   So do I too, if it be not too much. Brings a
120   victory in his pocket? The wounds become him.

VOLUMNIA   On's brows. Menenius, he comes the third
   time home with the oaken garland.

MENENIUS   Has he disciplined Aufidius soundly?

VOLUMNIA   Titus Lartius writes they fought together,
   but Aufidius got off.

MENENIUS   And 'twas time for him too, I'll warrant him
   that. An he had stayed by him, I would not have been
128   so fidiused for all the chests in Corioles and the gold
129   that's in them. Is the Senate possessed of this?

130 VOLUMNIA   Good ladies, let's go. Yes, yes, yes! The Senate has letters from the general, wherein he gives my
132   son the whole name of the war. He hath in this action
   outdone his former deeds doubly.

---

102 *Take . . . Jupiter* i.e., I throw my cap in the air   112 *make a lip at* mock
113 *sovereign* efficacious; *Galen* Greek medical authority   114 *empiricutic*
quackish; *to* compared to   115 *drench* dose   119 *a* he (familiar)   128 *fidiused* treated like Aufidius   129 *possessed* fully informed   132 *name* credit

VALERIA   In troth, there's wondrous things spoke of him.   134
MENENIUS   Wondrous? Ay, I warrant you, and not without his true purchasing.   136
VIRGILIA   The gods grant them true!
VOLUMNIA   True? pow waw!   138
MENENIUS   True? I'll be sworn they are true. Where is he
wounded? *[To the Tribunes]* God save your good wor-   140
ships! Martius is coming home. He has more cause to
be proud. – Where is he wounded?
VOLUMNIA   I' th' shoulder and i' th' left arm. There will
be large cicatrices to show the people, when he shall   144
stand for his place. He received in the repulse of Tar-   145
quin seven hurts i' th' body.
MENENIUS   One i' th' neck and two i' th' thigh – there's
nine that I know.
VOLUMNIA   He had, before this last expedition, twenty-
five wounds upon him.   150
MENENIUS   Now it's twenty-seven. Every gash was an
enemy's grave. *[A shout and flourish.]* Hark! the trum-
pets.
VOLUMNIA
These are the ushers of Martius. Before him
He carries noise, and behind him he leaves tears.
Death, that dark spirit, in's nervy arm doth lie;   156
Which, being advanced, declines, and then men die.   157
        *A sennet. Trumpets sound. Enter Cominius the
        General and Titus Lartius; between them, Coriolanus,
        crowned with an oaken garland; with Captains and
        Soldiers and a Herald.*
HERALD
Know, Rome, that all alone Martius did fight
Within Corioles gates, where he hath won,

---

134 *troth* truth   136 *purchasing* earning   138 *pow waw* pooh   144 *cicatri-*
ces scars   145 *stand* be a candidate; *place* position (i.e., the consulship)
145–46 *Tarquin* deposed Roman tyrant   156 *nervy* sinewy   157 *advanced*
raised; *declines* sinks down   157 s.d. *sennet* trumpet signal

160   With fame, a name to Caius Martius. These
      In honor follows Coriolanus.
      Welcome to Rome, renownèd Coriolanus!
          Sound flourish.

ALL
      Welcome to Rome, renownèd Coriolanus!

CORIOLANUS
      No more of this; it does offend my heart.
      Pray now, no more.

COMINIUS   Look, sir, your mother.

CORIOLANUS   O,
      You have, I know, petitioned all the gods
167   For my prosperity!
          Kneels.

VOLUMNIA   Nay, my good soldier, up.
      My gentle Martius, worthy Caius, and
169   By deed-achieving honor newly named –
170   What is it? – Coriolanus must I call thee? –
      But, O, thy wife!

CORIOLANUS   My gracious silence, hail!
      Wouldst thou have laughed had I come coffined home,
      That weep'st to see me triumph? Ah, my dear,
      Such eyes the widows in Corioles wear,
      And mothers that lack sons.

MENENIUS   Now, the gods crown thee!

CORIOLANUS
      And live you yet? *[To Valeria]* O my sweet lady, pardon.

VOLUMNIA
      I know not where to turn. O, welcome home!
      And welcome, general! And you're welcome all!

MENENIUS
      A hundred thousand welcomes! I could weep
180   And I could laugh; I am light and heavy. Welcome!
181   A curse begin at very root on's heart

---

160 *With* along with; *to* in addition to **167** *prosperity* success **169** *deed-achieving* achieved by deeds **180** *light* joyful; *heavy* sad **181** *begin at* penetrate to; *on's* of his

That is not glad to see thee! You are three
That Rome should dote on; yet, by the faith of men,
We have some old crab trees here at home that will not
Be grafted to your relish. Yet welcome, warriors!   185
We call a nettle but a nettle and
The faults of fools but folly.

COMINIUS   Ever right.

CORIOLANUS
Menenius, ever, ever.   188

HERALD
Give way there, and go on!

CORIOLANUS   *[To Volumnia and Virgilia]*
                              Your hand, and yours.
Ere in our own house I do shade my head,   190
The good patricians must be visited;
From whom I have received not only greetings,
But with them change of honors.   193

VOLUMNIA   I have lived
To see inherited my very wishes   194
And the buildings of my fancy. Only   195
There's one thing wanting, which I doubt not but   196
Our Rome will cast upon thee.

CORIOLANUS   Know, good mother,
I had rather be their servant in my way,
Than sway with them in theirs.   199

COMINIUS   On, to the Capitol!
  *Flourish. Cornets. Exeunt in state, as before. Brutus
  and Sicinius [come forward].*

BRUTUS
All tongues speak of him, and the bleared sights   200
Are spectacled to see him. Your prattling nurse
Into a rapture lets her baby cry,   202
While she chats him; the kitchen malkin pins   203

---

185 *grafted to your relish* implanted with a liking for you   188 *ever* still the
same   193 *change of honors* promotion   194 *inherited* realized   195 *buildings of my fancy* imaginative visions   196 *wanting* lacking   199 *sway* rule
200 *sights* eyesights   202 *rapture* fit   203 *chats* gossips about; *malkin* maid

204 Her richest lockram 'bout her reechy neck,
205 Clamb'ring the walls to eye him. Stalls, bulks, windows
206 Are smothered up, leads filled, and ridges horsed
207 With variable complexions, all agreeing
208 In earnestness to see him. Seld-shown flamens
Do press among the popular throngs, and puff
210 To win a vulgar station. Our veiled dames
211 Commit the war of white and damask in
212 Their nicely guarded cheeks to th' wanton spoil
213 Of Phoebus' burning kisses – such a pother
As if that whatsoever god who leads him
215 Were slyly crept into his human powers
And gave him graceful posture.

SICINIUS   On the sudden,
217 I warrant him consul.

BRUTUS   Then our office may,
During his power, go sleep.

SICINIUS
219 He cannot temp'rately transport his honors
220 From where he should begin and end, but will
Lose those he hath won.

BRUTUS   In that there's comfort.

SICINIUS   Doubt not
The commoners, for whom we stand, but they
223 Upon their ancient malice will forget
With the least cause these his new honors, which
That he will give them make I as little question
226 As he is proud to do't.

BRUTUS   I heard him swear,
Were he to stand for consul, never would he

---

204 *lockram* coarse linen; *reechy* grimy 205 *bulks* shop fronts 206 *leads*
leaden roofs; *ridges horsed* rooftops bestridden 207 *variable complexions* different types 208 *Seld-shown flamens* priests who rarely appear 210 *vulgar
station* place in the crowd 211 *damask* red 212 *wanton spoil* lascivious rav-
ishment 213 *Phoebus* the sun; *pother* turmoil 215 *powers* faculties 217
consul one of Rome's two chief magistrates 219 *transport* carry 220 *and
end* to where he should end 223 *Upon . . . malice* because of their longstanding hostility 226 *As* as that

Appear i' th' marketplace nor on him put
The napless vesture of humility;   229
Nor, showing, as the manner is, his wounds   230
To th' people, beg their stinking breaths.
SICINIUS   'Tis right.
BRUTUS
It was his word. O, he would miss it rather
Than carry it but by the suit of the gentry to him   233
And the desire of the nobles.
SICINIUS   I wish no better
Than have him hold that purpose and to put it
In execution.   236
BRUTUS   'Tis most like he will.
SICINIUS
It shall be to him then as our good wills,   237
A sure destruction.
BRUTUS   So it must fall out
To him or our authorities for an end.   239
We must suggest the people in what hatred   240
He still hath held them; that to's power he would
Have made them mules, silenced their pleaders,
And dispropertied their freedoms, holding them,   243
In human action and capacity,
Of no more soul nor fitness for the world
Than camels in their war, who have their provand   246
Only for bearing burthens, and sore blows   247
For sinking under them.
SICINIUS   This, as you say, suggested
At sometime when his soaring insolence
Shall touch the people – which time shall not want,   250
If he be put upon't, and that's as easy   251
As to set dogs on sheep – will be his fire

---

229 *napless* threadbare   233 *carry* win   236 *like* likely   237 *good wills* advantage requires   239 *for* are at   240 *suggest* insinuate to   243 *dispropertied* dispossessed of   246 *provand* provender   247 *burthens* burdens   250 *which . . . want* and that time will come   251 *put upon't* provoked

To kindle their dry stubble; and their blaze
Shall darken him forever.
  Enter a Messenger.

BRUTUS   What's the matter?

MESSENGER
You are sent for to th' Capitol.
'Tis thought that Martius shall be consul.
I have seen the dumb men throng to see him,
And the blind to hear him speak. Matrons flung gloves,
259 Ladies and maids their scarfs and handkerchers,
260 Upon him as he passed. The nobles bended,
As to Jove's statue, and the commons made
A shower and thunder with their caps and shouts.
I never saw the like.

BRUTUS   Let's to the Capitol,
264 And carry with us ears and eyes for th' time,
265 But hearts for the event.

SICINIUS   Have with you.   *Exeunt.*

*

∾ **II.2** *Enter two Officers, to lay cushions, as it were in
the Capitol.*

FIRST OFFICER Come, come, they are almost here. How
many stand for consulships?

3 SECOND OFFICER Three, they say; but 'tis thought of
everyone Coriolanus will carry it.

5 FIRST OFFICER That's a brave fellow; but he's vengeance
proud, and loves not the common people.

SECOND OFFICER Faith, there hath been many great men
that have flattered the people who ne'er loved them;
and there be many that they have loved they know not
10 wherefore; so that, if they love they know not why, they

---

259 *handkerchers* handkerchiefs **264** *time* situation **265** *event* outcome
 II.2 The Roman senate house in the Capitol **s.d.** *cushions* used on stage
for seats **3** *of* by **5** *vengeance* terribly

hate upon no better a ground. Therefore, for Coriolanus neither to care whether they love or hate him manifests the true knowledge he has in their disposition, and out of his noble carelessness lets them plainly see't.

FIRST OFFICER   If he did not care whether he had their love or no, he waved indifferently 'twixt doing them neither good nor harm; but he seeks their hate with greater devotion than they can render it him, and leaves nothing undone that may fully discover him their opposite. Now to seem to affect the malice and displeasure of the people is as bad as that which he dislikes — to flatter them for their love.

SECOND OFFICER   He hath deserved worthily of his country; and his ascent is not by such easy degrees as those who, having been supple and courteous to the people, bonneted, without any further deed to have them at all into their estimation and report. But he hath so planted his honors in their eyes and his actions in their hearts that for their tongues to be silent and not confess so much were a kind of ingrateful injury. To report otherwise were a malice that, giving itself the lie, would pluck reproof and rebuke from every ear that heard it.

FIRST OFFICER   No more of him; he's a worthy man. Make way, they are coming.

A sennet. Enter the Patricians and the Tribunes of the People, Lictors before them: Coriolanus, Menenius, Cominius the Consul. Sicinius and Brutus take their places by themselves. Coriolanus stands.

MENENIUS
Having determined of the Volsces and

---

13 *in* of 14 *carelessness* indifference 16 *waved* wavered 20–21 *discover . . . opposite* show that he is opposed to them 21 *affect* cultivate 27–28 *bonneted . . . report* did nothing but doff their hats to attain popularity 36 s.d. *Lictors* magistrates' attendants 37 *determined of* concluded with

    To send for Titus Lartius, it remains,
39   As the main point of this our after-meeting,
40   To gratify his noble service that
    Hath thus stood for his country. Therefore, please you,
    Most reverend and grave elders, to desire
    The present consul, and last general
44   In our well-found successes, to report
    A little of that worthy work performed
    By Caius Martius Coriolanus, whom
    We met here both to thank and to remember
48   With honors like himself.
FIRST SENATOR   Speak, good Cominius.
    Leave nothing out for length, and make us think
50   Rather our state's defective for requital
51   Than we to stretch it out.
        [To the Tribunes]   Masters o' th' people,
    We do request your kindest ears, and after,
53   Your loving motion toward the common body
54   To yield what passes here.
SICINIUS   We are convented
55   Upon a pleasing treaty, and have hearts
    Inclinable to honor and advance
57   The theme of our assembly.
BRUTUS   Which the rather
58   We shall be blest to do if he remember
    A kinder value of the people than
60   He hath hereto prized them at.
MENENIUS   That's off, that's off!
    I would you rather had been silent. Please you
    To hear Cominius speak?

---

39 *after-meeting* later meeting 40 *gratify* requite 44 *well-found* fortunately
encountered 48 *like himself* fitting to him 50 *defective for requital* unable
to reward adequately 51 *stretch it out* extend it 53 *Your . . . body* your kind
mediation with the people 54 *yield* grant; *convented* summoned 55 *Upon*
to consider; *treaty* topic to be treated 57 *rather* sooner 58 *blest* happy 60
off beside the point

BRUTUS   Most willingly;
  But yet my caution was more pertinent
  Than the rebuke you give it.
MENENIUS   He loves your people;
  But tie him not to be their bedfellow.
  Worthy Cominius, speak.
      Coriolanus rises, and offers to go away.
                              Nay, keep your place.
FIRST SENATOR
  Sit, Coriolanus. Never shame to hear
  What you have nobly done.
CORIOLANUS   Your honors' pardon.
  I had rather have my wounds to heal again
  Than hear say how I got them.   70
BRUTUS   Sir, I hope
  My words disbenched you not.   71
CORIOLANUS   No, sir. Yet oft,
  When blows have made me stay, I fled from words.
  You soothed not, therefore hurt not. But your people, 72
  I love them as they weigh –
MENENIUS   Pray now, sit down.
CORIOLANUS
  I had rather have one scratch my head i' th' sun   74
  When the alarum were struck than idly sit
  To hear my nothings monstered.   *Exit.* 76
MENENIUS   Masters of the people,
  Your multiplying spawn how can he flatter –
  That's thousand to one good one – when you now see   78
  He'd rather venture all his limbs for honor
  Than one on's ears to hear it? Proceed, Cominius.   80
COMINIUS
  I shall lack voice. The deeds of Coriolanus

---

71 *disbenched you* made you get up 72 *soothed* flattered 74–75 *have . . . struck* i.e., be idle during battle 76 *monstered* made marvels of 78 *that's . . . one* i.e., there are a thousand worthless ones for every good one 80 *Than . . . hear it* than venture one of his ears to hear about it

Should not be uttered feebly. It is held
That valor is the chiefest virtue, and
Most dignifies the haver. If it be,
The man I speak of cannot in the world
86 Be singly counterpoised. At sixteen years,
87 When Tarquin made a head for Rome, he fought
88 Beyond the mark of others. Our then dictator,
Whom with all praise I point at, saw him fight,
90 When with his Amazonian chin he drove
91 The bristled lips before him. He bestrid
92 An o'erpressed Roman and i' th' consul's view
Slew three opposers. Tarquin's self he met,
94 And struck him on his knee. In that day's feats,
When he might act the woman in the scene,
96 He proved best man i' th' field, and for his meed
97 Was brow-bound with the oak. His pupil age
98 Man-entered thus, he waxèd like a sea,
And in the brunt of seventeen battles since
100 He lurched all swords of the garland. For this last,
Before and in Corioles, let me say
102 I cannot speak him home. He stopped the fliers,
And by his rare example made the coward
Turn terror into sport. As weeds before
A vessel under sail, so men obeyed
106 And fell below his stem. His sword, death's stamp,
Where it did mark, it took. From face to foot
He was a thing of blood, whose every motion
109 Was timed with dying cries. Alone he entered
110 The mortal gate of th' city, which he painted

---

86 *singly counterpoised* equaled by another individual   87 *made . . . for* raised an army to reconquer   88 *dictator* wartime leader   90 *Amazonian* unbearded (like a female warrior)   91 *bristled lips* i.e., adult men; *bestrid* protected   92 *o'erpressed* overwhelmed   94 *on* to   96 *meed* recompose   97 *Was . . . oak* was crowned with an oaken garland   98 *Man-entered* initiated into manhood; *waxèd* grew   100 *lurched* robbed   102 *speak him home* do him justice   106 *stem* bow   109 *timed* rhythmically accompanied   110 *mortal* fatal

With shunless destiny; aidless came off,   111
And with a sudden reinforcement struck
Corioles like a planet. Now all's his.
When by and by the din of war gan pierce   114
His ready sense, then straight his doubled spirit   115
Requickened what in flesh was fatigate,   116
And to the battle came he, where he did
Run reeking o'er the lives of men, as if   118
'Twere a perpetual spoil, and till we called   119
Both field and city ours, he never stood   120
To ease his breast with panting.
MENENIUS   Worthy man!
FIRST SENATOR
He cannot but with measure fit the honors   122
Which we devise him.   123
COMINIUS   Our spoils he kicked at,
And looked upon things precious as they were
The common muck of the world. He covets less
Than misery itself would give; rewards   126
His deeds with doing them; and is content
To spend the time to end it.   128
MENENIUS   He's right noble.
Let him be called for.
FIRST SENATOR   Call Coriolanus.
OFFICER
He doth appear.   130
    Enter Coriolanus.
MENENIUS
The Senate, Coriolanus, are well pleased
To make thee consul.
CORIOLANUS   I do owe them still
My life and services.

---

111 *shunless* inevitable 114 *gan* began to 115 *ready* alert; *doubled*
strengthened 116 *requickened* revived; *fatigate* weary 118 *reeking* steam-
ing 119 *perpetual spoil* endless slaughter 120 *stood* stopped 122 *with
measure* in proportion 123 *kicked at* spurned 126 *misery* poverty 128
spend . . . it pass his time in killing time

MENENIUS   It then remains
That you do speak to the people.
CORIOLANUS   I do beseech you,
Let me o'erleap that custom; for I cannot
136 Put on the gown, stand naked, and entreat them
137 For my wounds' sake to give their suffrage.
Please you that I may pass this doing.
SICINIUS   Sir, the people
139 Must have their voices; neither will they bate
140 One jot of ceremony.
MENENIUS   Put them not to't.
Pray you, go fit you to the custom and
Take to you, as your predecessors have,
143 Your honor with your form.
CORIOLANUS   It is a part
That I shall blush in acting, and might well
Be taken from the people.
BRUTUS *[To Sicinius]*   Mark you that?
CORIOLANUS
To brag unto them "Thus I did, and thus!"
Show them th' unaching scars which I should hide,
As if I had received them for the hire
149 Of their breath only!
MENENIUS   Do not stand upon't.
150 We recommend to you, tribunes of the people,
Our purpose to them; and to our noble consul
Wish we all joy and honor.
SENATORS
To Coriolanus come all joy and honor!
                    Flourish. Cornets. Then exeunt.
                    Manent Sicinius and Brutus.
BRUTUS
You see how he intends to use the people.
SICINIUS
155 May they perceive's intent! He will require them

---

136 *naked* exposed 137 *suffrage* votes 139 *voices* votes; *bate* abate 143
form formality 149 *stand* insist 150 *recommend* entrust 155 *require* ask

As if he did contemn what he requested   156
Should be in them to give.   157
BRUTUS   Come, we'll inform them
Of our proceedings here. On th' marketplace   158
I know they do attend us.   [Exeunt.]   159

                              *

❧ II.3 *Enter seven or eight Citizens.*

FIRST CITIZEN   Once if he do require our voices we ought   1
not to deny him.
SECOND CITIZEN   We may, sir, if we will.
THIRD CITIZEN   We have power in ourselves to do it, but   4
it is a power that we have no power to do. For if he   5
show us his wounds and tell us his deeds, we are to put
our tongues into those wounds and speak for them. So,
if he tell us his noble deeds, we must also tell him our
noble acceptance of them. Ingratitude is monstrous;
and for the multitude to be ingrateful were to make a   10
monster of the multitude; of the which we being members, should bring ourselves to be monstrous members.
FIRST CITIZEN   And to make us no better thought of, a   13
little help will serve; for once we stood up about the   14
corn, he himself stuck not to call us the many-headed   15
multitude.
THIRD CITIZEN   We have been called so of many, not that   17
our heads are some brown, some black, some abram,   18
some bald, but that our wits are so diversely colored;
and truly I think if all our wits were to issue out of one   20
skull, they would fly east, west, north, south, and their   21
consent of one direct way should be at once to all the
points o' th' compass.

---

156 *contemn* despise   157 *in them* in their power   158 *marketplace* the
Forum   159 *attend* await   II.3 The Roman Forum   1 *Once if* if and when
4 *power* authority   5 *no power* no right   13–14 *a little . . . serve* not much is
needed   14 *once* when   15 *stuck not* did not hesitate   17 *of* by   18 *abram*
auburn   21–23 *their . . . compass* their agreement to go one way would result in their flying off in every direction

SECOND CITIZEN Think you so? Which way do you
   judge my wit would fly?

THIRD CITIZEN Nay, your wit will not so soon out as another man's will; 'tis strongly wedged up in a block-
28 head. But if it were at liberty, 'twould, sure, southward.

SECOND CITIZEN Why that way?

30 THIRD CITIZEN To lose itself in a fog, where being three
31 parts melted away with rotten dews, the fourth would
   return for conscience sake to help get thee a wife.

33 SECOND CITIZEN You are never without your tricks. You
   may, you may!

THIRD CITIZEN Are you all resolved to give your voices?
36 But that's no matter, the greater part carries it. I say, if
   he would incline to the people, there was never a wor-
   thier man.

> *Enter Coriolanus in a gown of humility, with*
> *Menenius.*

Here he comes, and in the gown of humility. Mark his
40 behavior. We are not to stay all together, but to come
   by him where he stands, by ones, by twos, and by
42 threes. He's to make his requests by particulars; wherein
   every one of us has a single honor, in giving him our
   own voices with our own tongues. Therefore follow
   me, and I'll direct you how you shall go by him.

ALL Content, content.   *[Exeunt Citizens.]*

MENENIUS
  O sir, you are not right. Have you not known
  The worthiest men have done't?

CORIOLANUS   What must I say?
  "I pray, sir" – Plague upon't! I cannot bring
50 My tongue to such a pace. "Look, sir, my wounds.
  I got them in my country's service, when
  Some certain of your brethren roared and ran
  From th' noise of our own drums."

---

28 *southward* probably beginning an obscene joke continued through l. 32
31 *rotten* unwholesome 33 *tricks* jokes 33–34 *You may* go on 36 *greater
part* majority 42 *by particulars* to individuals

MENENIUS   O me, the gods!
  You must not speak of that. You must desire them
  To think upon you.
CORIOLANUS   Think upon me? Hang 'em!
  I would they would forget me, like the virtues
  Which our divines lose by 'em.   57
MENENIUS   You'll mar all.
  I'll leave you. Pray you, speak to 'em, I pray you,
  In wholesome manner.   *Exit.* 59
CORIOLANUS   Bid them wash their faces
  And keep their teeth clean.   60
      Enter three of the Citizens.
                            So, here comes a brace.
  You know the cause, sir, of my standing here.
THIRD CITIZEN   We do, sir. Tell us what hath brought
  you to't.
CORIOLANUS   Mine own desert.
SECOND CITIZEN   Your own desert?   65
CORIOLANUS   Ay, not mine own desire.
THIRD CITIZEN   How not your own desire?
CORIOLANUS   No, sir, 'twas never my desire yet to trou-
  ble the poor with begging.
THIRD CITIZEN   You must think, if we give you anything, 70
  we hope to gain by you.
CORIOLANUS   Well then, I pray, your price o' th' consul-
  ship?
FIRST CITIZEN   The price is to ask it kindly.
CORIOLANUS   Kindly, sir, I pray, let me ha't. I have
  wounds to show you, which shall be yours in private.   76
  Your good voice, sir. What say you?
SECOND CITIZEN   You shall ha't, worthy sir.
CORIOLANUS   A match, sir. There's in all two worthy   79
  voices begged. I have your alms. Adieu.   80
THIRD CITIZEN   But this is something odd.

---

57 *lose by* fail to inculcate in   59 *wholesome* decent   60 *brace* pair   65 *desert*
deserving   76 *yours* available to you   79 *match* agreement

82 SECOND CITIZEN An 'twere to give again – but 'tis no
matter. *Exeunt.*
   Enter two other Citizens.

84 CORIOLANUS Pray you now, if it may stand with the
tune of your voices that I may be consul, I have here
the customary gown.

FOURTH CITIZEN You have deserved nobly of your country, and you have not deserved nobly.

CORIOLANUS Your enigma?

90 FOURTH CITIZEN You have been a scourge to her ene-
91 mies; you have been a rod to her friends. You have not
indeed loved the common people.

CORIOLANUS You should account me the more virtuous
94 that I have not been common in my love. I will, sir,
95 flatter my sworn brother, the people, to earn a dearer
96 estimation of them. 'Tis a condition they account gentle; and since the wisdom of their choice is rather to
have my hat than my heart, I will practice the insinuat-
99 ing nod and be off to them most counterfeitly. That is,
100 sir, I will counterfeit the bewitchment of some popular
man and give it bountiful to the desirers. Therefore, beseech you, I may be consul.

FIFTH CITIZEN We hope to find you our friend, and
104 therefore give you our voices heartily.

FOURTH CITIZEN You have received many wounds for
your country.

107 CORIOLANUS I will not seal your knowledge with showing them. I will make much of your voices, and so trouble you no farther.

110 BOTH The gods give you joy, sir, heartily! *[Exeunt.]*
CORIOLANUS
   Most sweet voices!
   Better it is to die, better to starve,

---

82 *An 'twere* if it were 84 *stand* accord 91 *rod* stick to beat with 94 *common* promiscuous 95–96 *dearer estimation of* higher opinion from 96
condition quality; *gentle* amiable 99 *be off* take my hat off 100 *bewitchment* witchery 100–1 *popular man* man of the people 104 *heartily* whole-
heartedly 107 *seal* confirm

Than crave the hire which first we do deserve.	113
Why in this wolvish toge should I stand here,	114
To beg of Hob and Dick that does appear	115
Their needless vouches? Custom calls me to't.	116
What custom wills, in all things should we do't,	117
The dust on antique time would lie unswept	118
And mountainous error be too highly heaped	
For truth t' o'erpeer. Rather than fool it so,	120
Let the high office and the honor go	
To one that would do thus. I am half through;	
The one part suffered, the other will I do.	123

    Enter three Citizens more.

Here come moe voices.	124
Your voices! For your voices I have fought;	
Watched for your voices; for your voices bear	126
Of wounds two dozen odd; battles thrice six	
I have seen and heard of; for your voices	
Have done many things, some less, some more.	
Your voices! indeed, I would be consul.	*130*

SIXTH CITIZEN   He has done nobly, and cannot go without any honest man's voice.

SEVENTH CITIZEN   Therefore let him be consul. The gods give him joy, and make him good friend to the people!

ALL   Amen, amen. God save thee, noble consul!

                          [Exeunt.]

CORIOLANUS   Worthy voices!

    Enter Menenius, with Brutus and Sicinius.

MENENIUS

You have stood your limitation, and the tribunes	138
Endue you with the people's voice. Remains	139

---

113 *hire* reward; *first* beforehand   114 *toge* toga   115 *Hob* (rustic nickname for Robert); *that does appear* as they come by   116 *vouches* attestations   117 *should we do't* if we did it   118 *antique* ancient   120 *o'erpeer* overtop; *fool it* play the fool   123 *suffered* endured   124 *moe* more   126 *Watched* stayed awake   138 *limitation* appointed time   139 *Endue* endow; *Remains* it remains

140   That, in th' official marks invested, you
       Anon do meet the Senate.
CORIOLANUS   Is this done?
SICINIUS
       The custom of request you have discharged.
       The people do admit you, and are summoned
144   To meet anon upon your approbation.
CORIOLANUS
       Where? at the Senate House?
SICINIUS   There, Coriolanus.
CORIOLANUS
       May I change these garments?
SICINIUS   You may, sir.
CORIOLANUS
       That I'll straight do; and, knowing myself again,
       Repair to th' Senate House.
MENENIUS
149   I'll keep you company. Will you along?
BRUTUS
150   We stay here for the people.
SICINIUS   Fare you well.
                        Exeunt Coriolanus and Menenius.
       He has it now, and by his looks, methinks,
       'Tis warm at's heart.
BRUTUS
       With a proud heart he wore his humble weeds.
       Will you dismiss the people?
           Enter the Plebeians.
SICINIUS
155   How now, my masters! Have you chose this man?
FIRST CITIZEN
       He has our voices, sir.
BRUTUS
       We pray the gods he may deserve your loves.

---

140 *official marks* insignia   144 *upon your approbation* to confirm your election   149 *along* come along   155 *my masters* gentlemen

SECOND CITIZEN
  Amen, sir. To my poor unworthy notice,
  He mocked us when he begged our voices.
THIRD CITIZEN   Certainly
  He flouted us downright.   *160*
FIRST CITIZEN
  No, 'tis his kind of speech; he did not mock us.
SECOND CITIZEN
  Not one amongst us, save yourself, but says
  He used us scornfully. He should have showed us
  His marks of merit, wounds received for's country.   *164*
SICINIUS
  Why, so he did, I am sure.
ALL   No, no! No man saw 'em.
THIRD CITIZEN
  He said he had wounds, which he could show in private;
  And with his hat, thus waving it in scorn,
  "I would be consul," says he. "Aged custom,   *168*
  But by your voices, will not so permit me.
  Your voices therefore." When we granted that,   *170*
  Here was "I thank you for your voices, thank you!
  Your most sweet voices! Now you have left your voices,
  I have no further with you." Was not this mockery?   *173*
SICINIUS
  Why either were you ignorant to see it,   *174*
  Or, seeing it, of such childish friendliness
  To yield your voices?
BRUTUS   Could you not have told him
  As you were lessoned? When he had no power,   *177*
  But was a petty servant to the state,
  He was your enemy, ever spake against
  Your liberties and the charters that you bear   *180*
  I' th' body of the weal; and now, arriving   *181*

---

164 *for's* for his   168 *Aged* ancient   173 *no further* nothing further to do
174 *ignorant* too unobservant   177 *lessoned* taught   180 *charters* rights
181 *body of the weal* commonwealth; *arriving* attaining

A place of potency and sway o' th' state,
If he should still malignantly remain
184   Fast foe to th' plebeii, your voices might
Be curses to yourselves. You should have said
That as his worthy deeds did claim no less
Than what he stood for, so his gracious nature
188   Would think upon you for your voices and
189   Translate his malice towards you into love,
190   Standing your friendly lord.

SICINIUS   Thus to have said,
191   As you were fore-advised, had touched his spirit
And tried his inclination; from him plucked
Either his gracious promise, which you might,
194   As cause had called you up, have held him to;
195   Or else it would have galled his surly nature,
196   Which easily endures not article
Tying him to aught. So putting him to rage,
198   You should have ta'en the advantage of his choler
And passed him unelected.

BRUTUS   Did you perceive
200   He did solicit you in free contempt
When he did need your loves, and do you think
That his contempt shall not be bruising to you
When he hath power to crush? Why, had your bodies
204   No heart among you? Or had you tongues to cry
205   Against the rectorship of judgment?

SICINIUS   Have you,
Ere now, denied the asker? And now again,
207   Of him that did not ask but mock, bestow
208   Your sued-for tongues!

THIRD CITIZEN
He's not confirmed; we may deny him yet.

_____

184 *plebeii* plebeians (Latin)   188 *Would think upon* should remember
189 *Translate* change   190 *Standing* steadfastly remaining   191 *fore-advised*
previously advised; *had* would have   194 *As . . . up* as occasion aroused you
195 *galled* exasperated   196–97 *article . . . aught* any conditions   198
choler fury   200 *free* open   204 *heart* courage; *cry* protest   205 *rectorship*
rule   207 *Of* on; *bestow* to bestow   208 *sued-for* solicited

SECOND CITIZEN
  And will deny him.   210
  I'll have five hundred voices of that sound.

FIRST CITIZEN
  I twice five hundred, and their friends to piece 'em.   212

BRUTUS
  Get you hence instantly, and tell those friends
  They have chose a consul that will from them take
  Their liberties; make them of no more voice
  Than dogs, that are as often beat for barking
  As therefore kept to do so.   217

SICINIUS   Let them assemble,
  And on a safer judgment all revoke
  Your ignorant election. Enforce his pride,   219
  And his old hate unto you. Besides, forget not   220
  With what contempt he wore the humble weed,   221
  How in his suit he scorned you; but your loves,
  Thinking upon his services, took from you
  Th' apprehension of his present portance,   224
  Which most gibingly, ungravely, he did fashion
  After th' inveterate hate he bears you.   226

BRUTUS   Lay
  A fault on us, your tribunes: that we labored,
  No impediment between, but that you must   228
  Cast your election on him.

SICINIUS   Say you chose him
  More after our commandment than as guided   230
  By your own true affections, and that your minds,   231
  Preoccupied with what you rather must do
  Than what you should, made you against the grain
  To voice him consul. Lay the fault on us.   234

BRUTUS
  Ay, spare us not. Say we read lectures to you,

---

212 *piece* supplement   **217** *therefore* for that reason   **219** *Enforce* emphasize
220 *forget not* do not ignore   **221** *weed* apparel   **224** *apprehension* observation; *portance* bearing   **226–27** *Lay . . . on* blame   **228** *No impediment between* that there should be no obstacle   **230** *after* according to   **231** *affections* inclinations   **234** *voice* vote

How youngly he began to serve his country,
How long continued, and what stock he springs of,
The noble house o' th' Martians, from whence came
239 That Ancus Martius, Numa's daughter's son,
240 Who after great Hostilius here was king;
Of the same house Publius and Quintus were,
242 That our best water brought by conduits hither;
And [Censorinus,] nobly namèd so,
244 Twice being [by the people chosen] censor,
Was his great ancestor.

SICINIUS   One thus descended,
That hath beside well in his person wrought
To be set high in place, we did commend
To your remembrances; but you have found,
249 Scaling his present bearing with his past,
250 That he's your fixèd enemy, and revoke
251 Your sudden approbation.

BRUTUS   Say, you ne'er had done't –
252 Harp on that still – but by our putting on;
253 And presently, when you have drawn your number,
Repair to th' Capitol.

ALL   We will so: almost all
Repent in their election.   *Exeunt Plebeians.*

BRUTUS   Let them go on.
256 This mutiny were better put in hazard
257 Than stay past doubt, for greater.
If, as his nature is, he fall in rage
259 With their refusal, both observe and answer
260 The vantage of his anger.

SICINIUS   To th' Capitol, come.
We will be there before the stream o' th' people,

---

239 *Numa* second king of Rome **242** *conduits* aqueducts **244** *censor*
keeper of public records **249** *Scaling* weighing **251** *sudden* hasty **252**
putting on instigation **253** *presently* immediately; *drawn your number* gath-
ered a crowd **256** *put in hazard* risked **257** *for greater* and run a greater
risk **259–60** *answer The vantage* take advantage

And this shall seem, as partly 'tis, their own,
Which we have goaded onward.   *Exeunt.*

*

∾ **III.1** *Cornets. Enter Coriolanus, Menenius, all the
Gentry, Cominius, Titus Lartius, and other Senators.*

CORIOLANUS
  Tullus Aufidius then had made new head?   1
LARTIUS
  He had, my lord, and that it was which caused
  Our swifter composition.   3
CORIOLANUS
  So then the Volsces stand but as at first,
  Ready, when time shall prompt them, to make road   5
  Upon's again.   6
COMINIUS   They are worn, lord consul, so,
  That we shall hardly in our ages see   7
  Their banners wave again.
CORIOLANUS   Saw you Aufidius?
LARTIUS
  On safeguard he came to me; and did curse   9
  Against the Volsces, for they had so vilely   10
  Yielded the town. He is retired to Antium.   11
CORIOLANUS
  Spoke he of me?
LARTIUS   He did, my lord.
CORIOLANUS   How? what?
LARTIUS
  How often he had met you, sword to sword;
  That of all things upon the earth he hated
  Your person most; that he would pawn his fortunes

III.1 A Roman street   1 *made new head* raised another army   3 *swifter composition* coming to terms the more speedily   5 *road* inroads   6 *worn* ex-
hausted   7 *ages* lifetimes   9 *safeguard* safe-conduct   10 *for* because   11
Yielded surrendered; *Antium* (Volscian capital)

16 To hopeless restitution, so he might
    Be called your vanquisher.

CORIOLANUS   At Antium lives he?

LARTIUS
    At Antium.

CORIOLANUS
    I wish I had a cause to seek him there,
20 To oppose his hatred fully. Welcome home.
        Enter Sicinius and Brutus.
    Behold, these are the tribunes of the people,
    The tongues o' th' common mouth. I do despise them,
23 For they do prank them in authority
24 Against all noble sufferance.

SICINIUS   Pass no further.

CORIOLANUS
    Ha! What is that?

BRUTUS
    It will be dangerous to go on. No further.

CORIOLANUS
    What makes this change?

MENENIUS
    The matter?

COMINIUS
29 Hath he not passed the noble and the common?

BRUTUS
30 Cominius, no.

CORIOLANUS   Have I had children's voices?

FIRST SENATOR
    Tribunes, give way. He shall to th' marketplace.

BRUTUS
    The people are incensed against him.

SICINIUS   Stop,
33 Or all will fall in broil.

---

16 *To hopeless restitution* beyond hope of recovery 23 *prank* dress up 24 *noble sufferance* patrician endurance 29 *passed* been approved by 33 *broil* conflict

CORIOLANUS   Are these your herd?
  Must these have voices, that can yield them now
  And straight disclaim their tongues? What are your   35
    offices?
  You being their mouths, why rule you not their teeth?   36
  Have you not set them on?
MENENIUS   Be calm, be calm.
CORIOLANUS
  It is a purposed thing, and grows by plot,   38
  To curb the will of the nobility.
  Suffer't, and live with such as cannot rule   40
  Nor ever will be ruled.
BRUTUS   Call't not a plot.
  The people cry you mocked them, and of late,
  When corn was given them gratis, you repined,   43
  Scandaled the suppliants for the people, called them   44
  Time-pleasers, flatterers, foes to nobleness.   45
CORIOLANUS
  Why, this was known before.
BRUTUS   Not to them all.
CORIOLANUS
  Have you informed them sithence?   47
BRUTUS   How! I inform them!
CORIOLANUS
  You are like to do such business.
BRUTUS   Not unlike,
  Each way, to better yours.   49
CORIOLANUS
  Why then should I be consul? By yond clouds,   50
  Let me deserve so ill as you, and make me
  Your fellow tribune.
SICINIUS   You show too much of that
  For which the people stir. If you will pass   53

------

35 *offices* duties 36 *rule* control 38 *purposed* calculated 40 *Suffer't* toler-
ate it; *live* you will live 43 *gratis* free; *repined* expressed regret 44 *Scandaled* defamed 45 *nobleness* aristocracy 47 *sithence* since 49 *better yours*
do better than you would do as consul 53 *For . . . stir* which disturbs the
people

To where you are bound, you must inquire your way,
55 Which you are out of, with a gentler spirit,
Or never be so noble as a consul,
57 Nor yoke with him for tribune.
MENENIUS   Let's be calm.
COMINIUS
58 The people are abused, set on. This paltering
Becomes not Rome, nor has Coriolanus
60 Deserved this so dishonored rub, laid falsely
I' th' plain way of his merit.
CORIOLANUS   Tell me of corn!
This was my speech, and I will speak't again –
MENENIUS
Not now, not now.
FIRST SENATOR   Not in this heat, sir, now.
CORIOLANUS
Now, as I live, I will.
My nobler friends, I crave their pardons.
66 For the mutable, rank-scented meiny,
67 Let them regard me as I do not flatter,
And therein behold themselves. I say again,
69 In soothing them we nourish 'gainst our Senate
70 The cockle of rebellion, insolence, sedition,
Which we ourselves have plowed for, sowed, and
    scattered
72 By mingling them with us, the honored number,
Who lack not virtue, no, nor power, but that
Which they have given to beggars.
MENENIUS   Well, no more.
FIRST SENATOR
No more words, we beseech you.
CORIOLANUS   How? no more?
As for my country I have shed my blood,

---

55 *are out of* have strayed from   57 *yoke* cooperate   58 *abused* deceived;
paltering equivocating   60 *dishonored rub* shameful obstacle   66 *For* as for;
meiny multitude   67–68 *regard . . . themselves* attend to me insofar as I do
not flatter, and see themselves as they are   69 *soothing* placating   70 *cockle*
weed   72 *honored* honorable

Not fearing outward force, so shall my lungs
Coin words till their decay against those measles   78
Which we disdain should tetter us, yet sought   79
The very way to catch them.   80
BRUTUS   You speak o' th' people
  As if you were a god to punish, not
  A man of their infirmity.
SICINIUS   'Twere well we let the people know't.
MENENIUS   What, what? His choler?
CORIOLANUS
  Choler! Were I as patient as the midnight sleep,
  By Jove, 'twould be my mind!   85
SICINIUS   It is a mind
  That shall remain a poison where it is,
  Not poison any further.
CORIOLANUS   Shall remain!
  Hear you this Triton of the minnows? Mark you   88
  His absolute "shall"?   89
COMINIUS   'Twas from the canon.
CORIOLANUS   "Shall"?
  O good but most unwise patricians! Why,   90
  You grave but reckless senators, have you thus
  Given Hydra here to choose an officer,   92
  That with his peremptory "shall," being but
  The horn and noise o' th' monster's, wants not spirit   94
  To say he'll turn your current in a ditch,
  And make your channel his? If he have power,
  Then vail your ignorance; if none, awake   97
  Your dangerous lenity. If you are learned,   98
  Be not as common fools; if you are not,
  Let them have cushions by you. You are plebeians   100
  If they be senators; and they are no less

---

78 *those measles* that leprosy   79 *tetter* break out in; *sought* have sought   85
my mind my opinion   88 *Triton* god who calms the waves   89 *from the*
canon out of order   92 *Given* allowed; *Hydra* many-headed monster   94
horn (attribute of Triton); *wants not spirit* doesn't lack the nerve   97 *vail*
your ignorance let your negligence bow down   98 *lenity* mildness   100 *have*
cushions by you sit with you in the senate

102   When, both your voices blended, the great'st taste
103   Most palates theirs. They choose their magistrate,
       And such a one as he, who puts his "shall,"
105   His popular "shall," against a graver bench
       Than ever frowned in Greece. By Jove himself,
       It makes the consuls base, and my soul aches
108   To know, when two authorities are up,
       Neither supreme, how soon confusion
110   May enter 'twixt the gap of both and take
       The one by th' other.

COMINIUS   Well, on to th' marketplace.

CORIOLANUS
       Whoever gave that counsel, to give forth
113   The corn o' th' storehouse gratis, as 'twas used
       Sometime in Greece –

MENENIUS   Well, well, no more of that.

CORIOLANUS
       Though there the people had more absolute power –
       I say they nourished disobedience, fed
       The ruin of the state.

BRUTUS   Why, shall the people give
       One that speaks thus their voice?

CORIOLANUS   I'll give my reasons,
       More worthier than their voices. They know the corn
120   Was not our recompense, resting well assured
121   They ne'er did service for't. Being pressed to th' war,
122   Even when the navel of the state was touched,
123   They would not thread the gates. This kind of service
       Did not deserve corn gratis. Being i' th' war,
       Their mutinies and revolts, wherein they showed
       Most valor, spoke not for them. Th' accusation
       Which they have often made against the Senate,
128   All cause unborn, could never be the native

---

102 *great'st taste* taste of the greatest   103 *palates* smacks of   105 *bench* leg-
islature   108 *up* in action   113 *as 'twas used* as the practice was   120 *recompense* reward to them   121 *pressed* conscripted   122 *navel* center   123
thread pass through   128 *All cause unborn* without justification; *native*
origin

Of our so frank donation. Well, what then?   129
How shall this bosom multiplied digest   130
The Senate's courtesy? Let deeds express
What's like to be their words: "We did request it;   132
We are the greater poll, and in true fear   133
They gave us our demands." Thus we debase
The nature of our seats, and make the rabble   135
Call our cares fears; which will in time
Break ope the locks o' th' Senate, and bring in
The crows to peck the eagles.
MENENIUS   Come, enough.
BRUTUS
  Enough, with overmeasure.
CORIOLANUS   No, take more!
What may be sworn by, both divine and human,   *140*
Seal what I end withal! This double worship,   141
Where one part does disdain with cause, the other
Insult without all reason; where gentry, title, wisdom,   143
Cannot conclude but by the yea and no
Of general ignorance – it must omit   145
Real necessities, and give way the while
To unstable slightness. Purpose so barred, it follows   147
Nothing is done to purpose. Therefore, beseech you –
You that will be less fearful than discreet;   149
That love the fundamental part of state   150
More than you doubt the change on't; that prefer   151
A noble life before a long, and wish
To jump a body with a dangerous physic   153
That's sure of death without it – at once pluck out
The multitudinous tongue; let them not lick
The sweet which is their poison. Your dishonor   156

---

129 *frank* free   **130** *bosom multiplied* many-breasted crowd   **132** *like* likely
133 *greater poll* majority   **135** *seats* positions of eminence   **141** *Seal* confirm; *withal* with; *double worship* divided authority   **143** *without* beyond
145 *omit* neglect   **147** *slightness* frivolity; *Purpose so barred* when planning
thus becomes impossible   **149** *discreet* wise   **150** *fundamental part* original
form   **151** *doubt* fear   **153** *jump* risk; *physic* medicine   **156** *sweet* flattery;
Your dishonor your being dishonored

Mangles true judgment, and bereaves the state
158 Of that integrity which should become't,
Not having the power to do the good it would
160 For th' ill which doth control't.
BRUTUS   'Has said enough.
SICINIUS
161 'Has spoken like a traitor, and shall answer
162 As traitors do.
CORIOLANUS   Thou wretch, despite o'erwhelm thee!
163 What should the people do with these bald tribunes
On whom depending, their obedience fails
165 To th' greater bench? In a rebellion,
166 When what's not meet, but what must be, was law,
Then were they chosen. In a better hour,
168 Let what is meet be said it must be meet,
And throw their power i' th dust.
BRUTUS
170 Manifest treason!
SICINIUS   This is a consul? No.
BRUTUS
171 The aediles, ho!
        Enter an Aedile.
                          Let him be apprehended.
SICINIUS
Go, call the people; *[Exit Aedile.]* in whose name myself
173 Attach thee as a traitorous innovator,
A foe to th' public weal. Obey, I charge thee,
175 And follow to thine answer.
CORIOLANUS   Hence, old goat!
ALL [PATRICIANS]
178 We'll surety him.
COMINIUS   Ag'd sir, hands off.

---

158 *integrity* wholeness; *become't* befit it   **160** *control't* overbear it;   *'Has* he
has   **161** *answer* pay the penalty   **162** *despite* scorn   **163** *What . . . do with*
why should the people have   **165** *greater bench* Senate   **166** *meet* proper
168 *Let . . . be meet* let it be said that what is proper should be done   **171**
aediles police officers   **173** *Attach* arrest; *innovator* political radical   **175** *an-*
swer interrogation   **178** *surety* stand pledged for

CORIOLANUS
    Hence, rotten thing! or I shall shake thy bones
    Out of thy garments.   180
SICINIUS   Help ye, citizens!
    Enter a rabble of Plebeians, with the Aediles.
MENENIUS
    On both sides more respect.
SICINIUS
    Here's he that would take from you all your power.
BRUTUS
    Seize him, aediles!
ALL [PLEBEIANS]
    Down with him! down with him!
SECOND SENATOR
    Weapons, weapons, weapons!
        They all bustle about Coriolanus.
ALL
    Tribunes! – Patricians! – Citizens! – What, ho!
    Sicinius! – Brutus! – Coriolanus! – Citizens!
    Peace, peace, peace! – Stay, hold, peace!
MENENIUS
    What is about to be? I am out of breath;
    Confusion's near; I cannot speak. You, tribunes   190
    To th' people! – Coriolanus, patience! –
    Speak, good Sicinius.
SICINIUS   Hear me, people. Peace!
ALL [PLEBEIANS]   Let's hear our tribune. Peace! Speak,
    speak, speak!
SICINIUS
    You are at point to lose your liberties.   195
    Martius would have all from you, Martius,
    Whom late you have named for consul.
MENENIUS   Fie, fie, fie!
    This is the way to kindle, not to quench.
FIRST SENATOR
    To unbuild the city and to lay all flat.

---

190 *Confusion* ruin   195 *at point to lose* on the point of losing

SICINIUS

200   What is the city but the people?

ALL [PLEBEIANS]   True,
    The people are the city.

BRUTUS
    By the consent of all we were established
    The people's magistrates.

ALL [PLEBEIANS]   You so remain.

MENENIUS
    And so are like to do.

COMINIUS
    That is the way to lay the city flat,
    To bring the roof to the foundation,
207   And bury all, which yet distinctly ranges,
    In heaps and piles of ruin.

SICINIUS   This deserves death.

BRUTUS
209   Or let us stand to our authority,
210   Or let us lose it. We do here pronounce,
    Upon the part o' th' people, in whose power
    We were elected theirs, Martius is worthy
213   Of present death.

SICINIUS   Therefore lay hold of him;
214   Bear him to th' rock Tarpeian, and from thence
    Into destruction cast him.

BRUTUS   Aediles, seize him!

ALL [PLEBEIANS]
    Yield, Martius, yield!

MENENIUS   Hear me one word.
    Beseech you, tribunes, hear me but a word.

AEDILES
    Peace, peace!

MENENIUS   *[To Brutus]*
    Be that you seem, truly your country's friend,

---

207 *distinctly ranges* is ranked hierarchically   209–10 *Or . . . or* either . . . or
213 *present* immediate   214 *rock Tarpeian* Capitoline cliff from which state
criminals were hurled

And temp'rately proceed to what you would   220
Thus violently redress.
BRUTUS   Sir, those cold ways,
That seem like prudent helps, are very poisonous
Where the disease is violent. Lay hands upon him,
And bear him to the rock.
    Coriolanus draws his sword.
CORIOLANUS   No, I'll die here.
There's some among you have beheld me fighting:
Come, try upon yourselves what you have seen me.
MENENIUS
Down with that sword! Tribunes, withdraw awhile.
BRUTUS
Lay hands upon him.
MENENIUS   Help Martius, help!
You that be noble, help him, young and old!
ALL [PLEBEIANS]
Down with him! down with him!   *Exeunt.*   230
    *In this mutiny the Tribunes, the Aediles, and the
    People are beat in.*
MENENIUS
Go, get you to your house! be gone, away!
All will be naught else.   232
SECOND SENATOR   Get you gone.
CORIOLANUS   Stand fast!
We have as many friends as enemies.
MENENIUS
  Shall it be put to that?
FIRST SENATOR   The gods forbid!
I prithee, noble friend, home to thy house;
Leave us to cure this cause.   236
MENENIUS   For 'tis a sore upon us
You cannot tent yourself. Be gone, beseech you.   237
COMINIUS
Come, sir, along with us.

_____
232 *naught* ruined   **236** *cause* disease   **237** *tent* treat

CORIOLANUS
   I would they were barbarians, as they are,
240   Though in Rome littered; not Romans, as they are not,
   Though calvèd i' th' porch o' th' Capitol —
MENENIUS   Be gone.
   Put not your worthy rage into your tongue.
243   One time will owe another.
CORIOLANUS   On fair ground
   I could beat forty of them.
MENENIUS   I could myself
245   Take up a brace o' th' best of them; yea, the two tribunes.
COMINIUS
   But now 'tis odds beyond arithmetic,
   And manhood is called foolery when it stands
248   Against a falling fabric. Will you hence
249   Before the tag return, whose rage doth rend
250   Like interrupted waters, and o'erbear
   What they are used to bear?
MENENIUS   Pray you, be gone.
252   I'll try whether my old wit be in request
   With those that have but little. This must be patched
   With cloth of any color.
COMINIUS   Nay, come away.
            Exeunt Coriolanus and Cominius [with others].
PATRICIAN
   This man has marred his fortune.
MENENIUS
   His nature is too noble for the world.
257   He would not flatter Neptune for his trident,
258   Or Jove for's power to thunder. His heart's his mouth.
   What his breast forges, that his tongue must vent;
260   And, being angry, does forget that ever
   He heard the name of death.

---

243 *One ... another* another time will make up for this   245 *Take up* cope
with   248 *fabric* building   249 *tag* rabble   250 *interrupted* obstructed; *o'erbear* overpower   252 *request* demand   257 *trident* three-pronged fork sym-
bolizing sea power   258 *His ... mouth* he speaks what he feels

 A noise within.
 Here's goodly work!
PATRICIAN   I would they were abed!
MENENIUS
 I would they were in Tiber! What the vengeance!
 Could he not speak 'em fair?   264
  Enter Brutus and Sicinius, with the Rabble again.
SICINIUS   Where is this viper
 That would depopulate the city and
 Be every man himself?   266
MENENIUS   You worthy tribunes –
SICINIUS
 He shall be thrown down the Tarpeian rock
 With rigorous hands. He hath resisted law,   268
 And therefore law shall scorn him further trial
 Than the severity of the public power,   270
 Which he so sets at nought.
FIRST CITIZEN   He shall well know
 The noble tribunes are the people's mouths,
 And we their hands.   273
ALL [PLEBEIANS]   He shall, sure on't.
MENENIUS   Sir, sir, –
SICINIUS
 Peace!
MENENIUS
 Do not cry havoc, where you should but hunt   275
 With modest warrant.   276
SICINIUS   Sir, how comes't that you
 Have holp to make this rescue?   277
MENENIUS   Hear me speak.
 As I do know the consul's worthiness,
 So can I name his faults –
SICINIUS   Consul! what consul?

---

264 *speak 'em fair* address them graciously 266 *Be . . . himself* constitute himself the whole population 268 *rigorous* pitiless 273 *sure on't* for certain 275 *cry havoc* call for slaughter 276 *modest* moderate 277 *holp* helped

MENENIUS
280   The consul Coriolanus.
BRUTUS   He consul!
ALL [PLEBEIANS]
   No, no, no, no, no!
MENENIUS
   If, by the tribunes' leave, and yours, good people,
   I may be heard, I would crave a word or two;
284   The which shall turn you to no further harm
   Than so much loss of time.
SICINIUS   Speak briefly then,
286   For we are peremptory to dispatch
   This viperous traitor. To eject him hence
288   Were but our danger, and to keep him here
   Our certain death. Therefore it is decreed
290   He dies tonight.
MENENIUS   Now the good gods forbid
   That our renownèd Rome, whose gratitude
292   Towards her deservèd children is enrolled
293   In Jove's own book, like an unnatural dam
   Should now eat up her own!
SICINIUS
   He's a disease that must be cut away.
MENENIUS
   O, he's a limb that has but a disease:
297   Mortal, to cut it off; to cure it, easy.
298   What has he done to Rome that's worthy death?
   Killing our enemies, the blood he hath lost –
300   Which, I dare vouch, is more than that he hath,
   By many an ounce – he dropped it for his country;
   And what is left, to lose it by his country
   Were to us all that do't and suffer it
304   A brand to th' end o' th' world.

---

284 *turn you to* cause you   286 *peremptory* resolved   288 *Were . . . danger*
would only place us at risk   292 *deservèd* meritorious   292–93 *enrolled . . .*
book recorded in the Capitol   293 *Jove* (another name for Jupiter); *dam*
mother   297 *mortal* fatal   298 *worthy* deserving of   300 *vouch* attest   304
brand mark of shame; *clean kam* quite wrong

SICINIUS   This is clean kam.
BRUTUS
  Merely awry. When he did love his country,   305
  It honored him.
SICINIUS   The service of the foot,
  Being once gangrened, is not then respected
  For what before it was.
BRUTUS   We'll hear no more.
  Pursue him to his house and pluck him thence,
  Lest his infection, being of catching nature,   310
  Spread further.
MENENIUS   One word more, one word.
  This tiger-footed rage, when it shall find
  The harm of unscanned swiftness, will too late   313
  Tie leaden pounds to's heels. Proceed by process,   314
  Lest parties, as he is beloved, break out   315
  And sack great Rome with Romans.
BRUTUS   If it were so –
SICINIUS
  What do ye talk?
  Have we not had a taste of his obedience?
  Our aediles smote? ourselves resisted? Come.   319
MENENIUS
  Consider this: he has been bred i' th' wars   320
  Since 'a could draw a sword, and is ill schooled
  In bolted language; meal and bran together   322
  He throws without distinction. Give me leave,
  I'll go to him and undertake to bring him
  Where he shall answer by a lawful form,   325
  In peace, to his utmost peril.
FIRST SENATOR   Noble tribunes,
  It is the humane way. The other course

---

305 *Merely awry* completely distorted   **313** *unscanned swiftness* thoughtless haste   **314** *to's* to its; *process* course of law   **315** *parties* factions   **319** *smote* smitten   **322** *bolted* sifted   **325–26** *answer . . . peril* peacefully face judgment, however severe

Will prove too bloody, and the end of it
Unknown to the beginning.

SICINIUS   Noble Menenius,
330   Be you then as the people's officer.
Masters, lay down your weapons.

BRUTUS   Go not home.

SICINIUS
332   Meet on the marketplace. We'll attend you there;
Where, if you bring not Martius, we'll proceed
In our first way.

MENENIUS   I'll bring him to you.
        [To the Senators]
Let me desire your company. He must come,
336   Or what is worst will follow.

FIRST SENATOR   Pray you, let's to him.
                                        Exeunt omnes.

                    *

∾ **III.2** *Enter Coriolanus, with Nobles.*

CORIOLANUS
Let them pull all about mine ears, present me
2   Death on the wheel or at wild horses' heels,
Or pile ten hills on the Tarpeian rock,
4   That the precipitation might down stretch
5   Below the beam of sight, yet will I still
Be thus to them.

NOBLE   You do the nobler.

CORIOLANUS
7   I muse my mother
Does not approve me further, who was wont
9   To call them woolen vassals, things created
10   To buy and sell with groats, to show bare heads

───────

332 *attend* await   336 *to* go to
  III.2 The house of Coriolanus   2 *wheel* instrument of torture   4 *precipitation* precipitousness   5 *Below . . . sight* beyond eyesight   7 *muse* wonder
that   9 *woolen vassals* underlings clothed in coarse woolen garments   10
groats fourpenny pieces

In congregations, to yawn, be still and wonder,   11
When one but of my ordinance stood up   12
To speak of peace or war.
    Enter Volumnia.   I talk of you:
Why did you wish me milder? Would you have me
False to my nature? Rather say I play
The man I am.
VOLUMNIA   O, sir, sir, sir,
I would have had you put your power well on,
Before you had worn it out.   18
CORIOLANUS   Let go.
VOLUMNIA
You might have been enough the man you are
With striving less to be so. Lesser had been   20
The taxings of your dispositions, if   21
You had not showed them how ye were disposed
Ere they lacked power to cross you.   23
CORIOLANUS   Let them hang!
VOLUMNIA
Ay, and burn too!
   Enter Menenius, with the Senators.

MENENIUS
Come, come, you have been too rough, something too   25
   rough.
You must return and mend it.
FIRST SENATOR   There's no remedy,
Unless, by not so doing, our good city
Cleave in the midst, and perish.   28
VOLUMNIA   Pray, be counseled.
I have a heart as little apt as yours,   29
But yet a brain that leads my use of anger   30
To better vantage.   31

---

11 *congregations* assemblies 12 *ordinance* rank 18 *Let go* desist 21 *taxings* condemnations; *dispositions* inclinations 23 *Ere they lacked* before they lost 25 *something* somewhat 28 *Cleave . . . midst* divide in the middle 29 *apt* compliant 31 *vantage* advantage

MENENIUS   Well said, noble woman!
Before he should thus stoop to th' herd, but that
33   The violent fit o' th' time craves it as physic
For the whole state, I would put mine armor on,
Which I can scarcely bear.
CORIOLANUS   What must I do?
MENENIUS
Return to th' tribunes.
CORIOLANUS   Well, what then? what then?
MENENIUS
Repent what you have spoke.
CORIOLANUS
For them? I cannot do it to the gods.
Must I then do't to them?
VOLUMNIA   You are too absolute,
40   Though therein you can never be too noble,
41   But when extremities speak. I have heard you say,
42   Honor and policy, like unsevered friends,
I' th' war do grow together. Grant that, and tell me
In peace what each of them by th' other lose
That they combine not there.
CORIOLANUS   Tush, tush!
MENENIUS   A good demand.
VOLUMNIA
If it be honor in your wars to seem
The same you are not – which for your best ends
48   You adopt your policy – how is it less or worse,
That it shall hold companionship in peace
50   With honor, as in war, since that to both
51   It stands in like request?
CORIOLANUS   Why force you this?
VOLUMNIA
52   Because that now it lies you on to speak

---

33 *physic* medicine   41 *extremities speak* dire necessity prompts   42 *policy*
strategy; *unsevered* inseparable   48 *adopt* adopt as   50–51 *since . . . request*
since it is equally necessary to both   51 *force* urge   52 *lies you on* is incum-
bent upon you

To th' people, not by your own instruction,
Nor by th' matter which your heart prompts you,
But with such words that are but roted in   55
Your tongue, though but bastards and syllables
Of no allowance to your bosom's truth.   57
Now, this no more dishonors you at all
Than to take in a town with gentle words,   59
Which else would put you to your fortune and   60
The hazard of much blood.
I would dissemble with my nature where
My fortunes and my friends at stake required
I should do so in honor. I am in this   64
Your wife, your son, these senators, the nobles;
And you will rather show our general louts   66
How you can frown than spend a fawn upon 'em,   67
For the inheritance of their loves and safeguard   68
Of what that want might ruin.   69
MENENIUS   Noble lady!
Come, go with us. Speak fair. You may salve so,   70
Not what is dangerous present, but the loss   71
Of what is past.
VOLUMNIA   I prithee now, my son,
Go to them, with this bonnet in thy hand;   73
And thus far having stretched it – here be with them –   74
Thy knee bussing the stones – for in such business   75
Action is eloquence, and the eyes of th' ignorant
More learned than the ears – waving thy head,   77
Which, often thus correcting thy stout heart,   78
Now humble as the ripest mulberry   79
That will not hold the handling; or say to them   80
Thou art their soldier, and being bred in broils   81

---

55 *roted* memorized   57 *Of . . . truth* unsanctioned by your real beliefs   59
take in capture   64 *am* speak for   66 *general* common   67 *fawn* flattering
appeal   68 *inheritance* obtainment   69 *that want* the lack of their loves
71–72 *Not . . . past* not only immediate danger but past loss   73 *bonnet* cap
74 *here . . . them* treat them thus   75 *bussing* kissing (vulgar)   77 *waving*
bowing   78 *correcting* chastening   79 *humble* abase   80 *hold* withstand
81 *broils* battles

Hast not the soft way which, thou dost confess,
Were fit for thee to use as they to claim,
In asking their good loves; but thou wilt frame
85 Thyself, forsooth, hereafter theirs, so far
86 As thou hast power and person.
MENENIUS   This but done,
87 Even as she speaks, why, their hearts were yours;
For they have pardons, being asked, as free
89 As words to little purpose.
VOLUMNIA   Prithee now,
90 Go, and be ruled, although I know thou hadst rather
91 Follow thine enemy in a fiery gulf
92 Than flatter him in a bower.
          Enter Cominius.   Here is Cominius.
COMINIUS
I have been i' th' marketplace; and, sir, 'tis fit
94 You make strong party, or defend yourself
By calmness or by absence. All's in anger.
MENENIUS
Only fair speech.
COMINIUS   I think 'twill serve, if he
Can thereto frame his spirit.
VOLUMNIA   He must, and will.
Prithee now, say you will, and go about it.
CORIOLANUS
99 Must I go show them my unbarbed sconce? Must I
100 With my base tongue give to my noble heart
A lie that it must bear? Well, I will do't.
102 Yet, were there but this single plot to lose,
103 This mold of Martius, they to dust should grind it
And throw't against the wind. To th' marketplace!
You have put me now to such a part which never
106 I shall discharge to th' life.

---

85 *forsooth* truly; *theirs* to suit them   86 *person* physical ability   87 *were*
would be   89 *words . . . purpose* a trifling concession   90 *ruled* advised   91
in into   92 *bower* boudoir   94 *make strong party* find strong allies   99 *unbarbed sconce* uncovered head   102 *plot* piece of earth (i.e., his body)   103
mold form   106 *discharge . . . life* enact convincingly

COMINIUS   Come, come, we'll prompt you.

VOLUMNIA

   I prithee now, sweet son, as thou hast said

   My praises made thee first a soldier, so,

   To have my praise for this, perform a part

   Thou hast not done before.   *110*

CORIOLANUS   Well, I must do't.

   Away, my disposition, and possess me

   Some harlot's spirit! My throat of war be turned,

   Which quired with my drum, into a pipe   113

   Small as an eunuch, or the virgin voice   114

   That babies lulls asleep! The smiles of knaves   115

   Tent in my cheeks, and schoolboys' tears take up   116

   The glasses of my sight! A beggar's tongue   117

   Make motion through my lips, and my armed knees,

   Who bowed but in my stirrup, bend like his

   That hath received an alms! I will not do't,   *120*

   Lest I surcease to honor mine own truth   121

   And by my body's action teach my mind

   A most inherent baseness.   123

VOLUMNIA   At thy choice, then.

   To beg of thee, it is my more dishonor

   Than thou of them. Come all to ruin! Let   125

   Thy mother rather feel thy pride than fear   126

   Thy dangerous stoutness, for I mock at death   127

   With as big heart as thou. Do as thou list.   128

   Thy valiantness was mine, thou suck'st it from me,

   But owe thy pride thyself.   *130*

CORIOLANUS   Pray, be content.

   Mother, I am going to the marketplace.

   Chide me no more. I'll mountebank their loves,   132

   Cog their hearts from them, and come home beloved   133

---

113 *quired* sang in chorus 114 *eunuch* castrated male (singer) 115 *babies
lulls* lulls dolls 116 *Tent* encamp; *take up* occupy 117 *glasses . . . sight* eye-
balls 121 *surcease* cease 123 *inherent* irremovable 125 *Than . . . them*
than for you to beg from them 126 *feel* suffer for 127 *dangerous stoutness*
danger provoked by your obstinacy 128 *thou list* you please 130 *owe* you
own 132 *mountebank* gain by artful speeches 133 *Cog* cheat

Of all the trades in Rome. Look, I am going.
Commend me to my wife. I'll return consul,
Or never trust to what my tongue can do
I' th' way of flattery further.

VOLUMNIA   Do your will.

                                          Exit Volumnia.

COMINIUS
Away! The tribunes do attend you. Arm yourself
To answer mildly, for they are prepared
140 With accusations, as I hear, more strong
Than are upon you yet.

CORIOLANUS
142 The word is "mildly." Pray you, let us go.
143 Let them accuse me by invention, I
144 Will answer in mine honor.

MENENIUS   Ay, but mildly.

CORIOLANUS
Well, mildly be't then. Mildly!   *Exeunt.*

                            *

∾ **III.3** *Enter Sicinius and Brutus.*

BRUTUS
1 In this point charge him home, that he affects
Tyrannical power. If he evade us there,
3 Enforce him with his envy to the people,
4 And that the spoil got on the Antiates
Was ne'er distributed.
       Enter an Aedile.   What, will he come?

AEDILE
He's coming.

BRUTUS   How accompanied?

---

142 *word* watchword 143 *accuse . . . invention* invent accusations against
me 144 *in* according to

III.3 The Roman Forum 1 *charge him home* press the charge against him;
affects aims at 3 *Enforce* confront; *envy to* ill will toward 4 *on* from

AEDILE
    With old Menenius, and those senators
    That always favored him.
SICINIUS   Have you a catalogue
    Of all the voices that we have procured
    Set down by th' poll?   10
AEDILE   I have; 'tis ready.
SICINIUS
    Have you collected them by tribes?
AEDILE   I have.
SICINIUS
    Assemble presently the people hither;
    And when they hear me say "It shall be so
    I' th' right and strength o' th' commons," be it either
    For death, for fine, or banishment, then let them,
    If I say "Fine," cry "Fine!" – if "Death," cry "Death!" –
    Insisting on the old prerogative   17
    And power i' th' truth o' th' cause.   18
AEDILE   I shall inform them.
BRUTUS
    And when such time they have begun to cry,   19
    Let them not cease, but with a din confused   20
    Enforce the present execution
    Of what we chance to sentence.
AEDILE   Very well.
SICINIUS
    Make them be strong, and ready for this hint   23
    When we shall hap to give't them.   24
BRUTUS   Go about it.
                                      [Exit Aedile.]
    Put him to choler straight. He hath been used   25
    Ever to conquer, and to have his worth   26

_____

10 *set . . . poll* recorded individually   17 *prerogative* established right   18
truth . . . cause justice of the case   19 *when such time* in such time as; *cry*
shout   23 *hint* cue   24 *hap* chance   25 *choler* rage   26–27 *worth of* full
power of

27 Of contradiction. Being once chafed, he cannot
Be reined again to temperance. Then he speaks
29 What's in his heart, and that is there which looks
30 With us to break his neck.

*Enter Coriolanus, Menenius, and Cominius, with
others.*

SICINIUS   Well, here he comes.

MENENIUS
Calmly, I do beseech you.

CORIOLANUS
32 Ay, as an ostler, that for th' poorest piece
33 Will bear the knave by th' volume. Th' honored gods
Keep Rome in safety, and the chairs of justice
Supplied with worthy men! plant love among's!
36 Throng our large temples with the shows of peace,
And not our streets with war!

FIRST SENATOR   Amen, amen.

MENENIUS
A noble wish.

Enter the Aedile, with the Plebeians.

SICINIUS
Draw near, ye people.

AEDILE
40 List to your tribunes. Audience! Peace, I say!

CORIOLANUS
First hear me speak.

BOTH TRIBUNES   Well, say. Peace, ho!

CORIOLANUS
42 Shall I be charged no further than this present?
43 Must all determine here?

SICINIUS   I do demand,
If you submit you to the people's voices,

---

27 *chafed* annoyed   29 *looks* seems likely   30 *With us* with our help   32
ostler stablehand at an inn; *piece* coin   33 *bear . . . volume* allow himself to
be called knave repeatedly   36 *shows* ceremonies   40 *List* listen; *Audience*
pay attention   42 *charged* obligated; *this present* the moment   43 *determine*
end

Allow their officers, and are content   45
To suffer lawful censure for such faults
As shall be proved upon you?
CORIOLANUS   I am content.
MENENIUS
Lo, citizens, he says he is content.
The warlike service he has done, consider; think
Upon the wounds his body bears, which show   50
Like graves i' th' holy churchyard.
CORIOLANUS   Scratches with briers,
Scars to move laughter only.
MENENIUS   Consider further,
That when he speaks not like a citizen,
You find him like a soldier. Do not take
His rougher accents for malicious sounds,
But, as I say, such as become a soldier,
Rather than envy you.   57
COMINIUS   Well, well, no more.
CORIOLANUS
What is the matter
That, being passed for consul with full voice,
I am so dishonored that the very hour   60
You take it off again?   61
SICINIUS   Answer to us.
CORIOLANUS
Say, then. 'Tis true, I ought so.   62
SICINIUS
We charge you that you have contrived to take
From Rome all seasoned office, and to wind   64
Yourself into a power tyrannical,
For which you are a traitor to the people.
CORIOLANUS
How? traitor?

---

45 *Allow* acknowledge 50 *Upon* about 57 *envy* show malice toward 61
Answer to us i.e., we will ask the questions 62 *so* to do so 64 *seasoned* established 64–65 *wind Yourself* insinuate yourself

MENENIUS   Nay, temperately! your promise.
CORIOLANUS
68   The fires i' th' lowest hell fold in the people!
69   Call me their traitor, thou injurious tribune!
70   Within thine eyes sat twenty thousand deaths,
      In thy hands clutched as many millions, in
      Thy lying tongue both numbers, I would say
      "Thou liest" unto thee with a voice as free
      As I do pray the gods.
SICINIUS   Mark you this, people?
ALL
      To th' rock, to th' rock with him!
SICINIUS   Peace!
      We need not put new matter to his charge.
      What you have seen him do and heard him speak,
      Beating your officers, cursing yourselves,
79   Opposing laws with strokes, and here defying
80   Those whose great power must try him – even this,
81   So criminal and in such capital kind,
      Deserves th' extremest death.
BRUTUS   But since he hath
      Served well for Rome –
CORIOLANUS   What do you prate of service?
BRUTUS
      I talk of that, that know it.
CORIOLANUS
      You?
MENENIUS
      Is this the promise that you made your mother?
COMINIUS
      Know, I pray you –
CORIOLANUS   I'll know no further.
      Let them pronounce the steep Tarpeian death,
89   Vagabond exile, flaying, pent to linger

---

68 *fold in* enfold   **69** *injurious* insulting   **70** *Within* if within   **79** *strokes* blows   **81** *capital* punishable by death   **89** *Vagabond* wandering; *flaying* being skinned alive; *pent* being confined

But with a grain a day – I would not buy   *90*
Their mercy at the price of one fair word;
Nor check my courage for what they can give,   *92*
To have't with saying "Good morrow."   *93*
SICINIUS   For that he has,
As much as in him lies, from time to time   *94*
Envied against the people, seeking means   *95*
To pluck away their power; as now at last   *96*
Given hostile strokes, and that not in the presence
Of dreaded justice, but on the ministers   *98*
That doth distribute it; i' th' name o' th' people
And in the power of us the tribunes, we,   *100*
Even from this instant, banish him our city,
In peril of precipitation   *102*
From off the rock Tarpeian, never more
To enter our Rome gates. I' th' people's name,
I say it shall be so.
ALL
It shall be so! it shall be so! Let him away!
He's banished, and it shall be so!
COMINIUS
Hear me, my masters, and my common friends –
SICINIUS
He's sentenced. No more hearing.
COMINIUS   Let me speak.
I have been consul, and can show for Rome   *110*
Her enemies' marks upon me. I do love
My country's good with a respect more tender,
More holy and profound, than mine own life,
My dear wife's estimate, her womb's increase,   *114*
And treasure of my loins. Then if I would
Speak that –
SICINIUS   We know your drift. Speak what?

---

92 *check* restrain **93** *For that* because **94** *in him lies* he could **95** *Envied against* shown ill will toward **96** *as* and because he has **98** *ministers* authorized agents **102** *precipitation* being thrown **114** *estimate* value; *increase* offspring

BRUTUS

117 There's no more to be said, but he is banished
As enemy to the people and his country.
It shall be so.

ALL

120 It shall be so! it shall be so!

CORIOLANUS

121 You common cry of curs, whose breath I hate
122 As reek o' th' rotten fens, whose loves I prize
As the dead carcasses of unburied men
That do corrupt my air, I banish you!
And here remain with your uncertainty.
Let every feeble rumor shake your hearts!
Your enemies, with nodding of their plumes,
Fan you into despair! Have the power still
To banish your defenders, till at length
130 Your ignorance – which finds not till it feels,
131 Making but reservation of yourselves;
Still your own foes – deliver you
133 As most abated captives to some nation
That won you without blows! Despising,
135 For you, the city, thus I turn my back.
There is a world elsewhere.

> *Exeunt Coriolanus, Cominius, with Menenius [and the other Senators].*

AEDILE

The people's enemy is gone, is gone!

ALL

Our enemy is banished! he is gone!
> *They all shout, and throw up their caps.*
>   Hoo! hoo!

SICINIUS

Go, see him out at gates, and follow him

---

117 *but* except that 121 *cry* pack 122 *reek* vapor; *fens* marshes 130 *finds . . . feels* learns only through experience 131 *Making . . . of* seeking to preserve only 133 *Abated* humbled 135 *For* because of

As he hath followed you, with all despite; 140
Give him deserved vexation. Let a guard 141
Attend us through the city.

ALL
Come, come, let's see him out at gates! Come.
The gods preserve our noble tribunes! Come. *Exeunt.*

*

∾ **IV.1** *Enter Coriolanus, Volumnia, Virgilia, Menenius,*
Cominius, with the young Nobility of Rome.

CORIOLANUS
Come, leave your tears. A brief farewell. The beast
With many heads butts me away. Nay, mother,
Where is your ancient courage? You were used 3
To say extremities was the trier of spirits;
That common chances common men could bear;
That when the sea was calm all boats alike
Showed mastership in floating; fortune's blows
When most struck home, being gentle wounded craves 8
A noble cunning. You were used to load me 9
With precepts that would make invincible 10
The heart that conned them. 11

VIRGILIA
O heavens! O heavens!

CORIOLANUS Nay, I prithee, woman –

VOLUMNIA
Now the red pestilence strike all trades in Rome, 13
And occupations perish!

CORIOLANUS What, what, what!
I shall be loved when I am lacked. Nay, mother, 15
Resume that spirit when you were wont to say,

---

140 *despite* disdain 141 *vexation* mortification
    IV.1 Before a gate of Rome 3 *ancient* earlier 8 *being . . . craves* to bear
one's wounds like a gentleman requires 9 *cunning* skill 11 *conned* studied
13 *red pestilence* typhus 15 *lacked* missed

If you had been the wife of Hercules,
Six of his labors you'd have done, and saved
Your husband so much sweat. Cominius,
20   Droop not; adieu. Farewell, my wife, my mother.
I'll do well yet. Thou old and true Menenius,
22   Thy tears are salter than a younger man's,
23   And venomous to thine eyes. My sometime general,
I have seen thee stern, and thou hast oft beheld
Heart-hard'ning spectacles. Tell these sad women
26   'Tis fond to wail inevitable strokes,
27   As 'tis to laugh at 'em. My mother, you wot well
28   My hazards still have been your solace, and –
29   Believe't not lightly – though I go alone,
30   Like to a lonely dragon that his fen
Makes feared and talked of more than seen, your son
32   Will or exceed the common or be caught
33   With cautelous baits and practice.
VOLUMNIA   My first son,
Whither wilt thou go? Take good Cominius
With thee awhile. Determine on some course
36   More than a wild exposture to each chance
37   That starts i' th' way before thee.
VIRGILIA   O the gods!
COMINIUS
I'll follow thee a month, devise with thee
Where thou shalt rest, that thou mayst hear of us
40   And we of thee. So, if the time thrust forth
41   A cause for thy repeal, we shall not send
O'er the vast world to seek a single man,
And lose advantage, which doth ever cool
I' th' absence of the needer.
CORIOLANUS   Fare ye well.
Thou hast years upon thee, and thou art too full

---

22 *salter* saltier   23 *sometime* former   26 *fond* foolish   27 *wot* know   28
still always   29 *Believe't . . . lightly* take my word for it   30 *fen* marsh   32
or . . . common either be exceptional   33 *cautelous* crafty; *practice* stratagem
36 *exposture* exposure   37 *starts* suddenly appears   41 *repeal* recall

Of the wars' surfeits to go rove with one   46
That's yet unbruised. Bring me but out at gate.   47
Come, my sweet wife, my dearest mother, and
My friends of noble touch. When I am forth,   49
Bid me farewell, and smile. I pray you, come.   50
While I remain above the ground, you shall
Hear from me still, and never of me aught
But what is like me formerly.

MENENIUS   That's worthily
As any ear can hear. Come, let's not weep.
If I could shake off but one seven-years
From these old arms and legs, by the good gods,
I'd with thee every foot.

CORIOLANUS   Give me thy hand.
Come.   *Exeunt.*

                                    *

∾ **IV.2** *Enter the two Tribunes, Sicinius and Brutus,*
      with the Aedile.

SICINIUS
Bid them all home. He's gone, and we'll no further.   1
The nobility are vexed, whom we see have sided
In his behalf.

BRUTUS   Now we have shown our power,
Let us seem humbler after it is done
Than when it was a-doing.   5

SICINIUS   Bid them home.
Say their great enemy is gone, and they
Stand in their ancient strength.   7

BRUTUS   Dismiss them home.
                                    [Exit Aedile.]

---

46 *surfeits* excesses 47 *Bring . . . gate* just accompany me to the gate 49
noble touch tested nobility
    IV.2 A street in Rome 1 *home* go home 5 *a-doing* being done 7 *ancient* previous

Here comes his mother.
SICINIUS   Let's not meet her.
BRUTUS   Why?
SICINIUS
  They say she's mad.
      Enter Volumnia, Virgilia, and Menenius.
BRUTUS
10   They have ta'en note of us. Keep on your way.
VOLUMNIA
11   O, you're well met. The hoarded plague o' th' gods
12   Requite your love!
MENENIUS   Peace, peace. Be not so loud.
VOLUMNIA
  If that I could for weeping, you should hear –
  Nay, and you shall hear some.
      [To Sicinius]   Will you be gone?
VIRGILIA   *[To Brutus]*
  You shall stay too. I would I had the power
16   To say so to my husband.
SICINIUS   Are you mankind?
VOLUMNIA
  Ay, fool, is that a shame? Note but this fool:
18   Was not a man my father? Hadst thou foxship
  To banish him that struck more blows for Rome
20   Than thou hast spoken words?
SICINIUS   O blessed heavens!
VOLUMNIA
21   Moe noble blows than ever thou wise words,
  And for Rome's good. I'll tell thee what – Yet go.
  Nay, but thou shalt stay too. I would my son
24   Were in Arabia, and thy tribe before him,
  His good sword in his hand.
SICINIUS   What then?
VIRGILIA   What then?
  He'd make an end of thy posterity.

---

11 *hoarded* accumulated 12 *Requite* reward 16 *mankind* masculine,
human 18 *foxship* animal cunning 21 *Moe* more 24 *Arabia* the desert

VOLUMNIA
Bastards and all.
Good man, the wounds that he does bear for Rome!

MENENIUS
Come, come, peace.

SICINIUS
I would he had continued to his country   30
As he began, and not unknit himself   31
The noble knot he made.

BRUTUS   I would he had.

VOLUMNIA
"I would he had"? 'Twas you incensed the rabble.
Cats, that can judge as fitly of his worth
As I can of those mysteries which heaven
Will not have earth to know!

BRUTUS   Pray, let us go.

VOLUMNIA
Now, pray, sir, get you gone.
You have done a brave deed. Ere you go, hear this:
As far as doth the Capitol exceed
The meanest house in Rome, so far my son –   40
This lady's husband here, this, do you see? –
Whom you have banished, does exceed you all.

BRUTUS
Well, well, we'll leave you.

SICINIUS   Why stay we to be baited
With one that wants her wits?   *Exeunt Tribunes.* 44

VOLUMNIA   Take my prayers with you.
I would the gods had nothing else to do
But to confirm my curses. Could I meet 'em   46
But once a day, it would unclog my heart
Of what lies heavy to't.   48

MENENIUS   You have told them home;
And, by my troth, you have cause. You'll sup with me? 49

31–32 *unknit . . . knot* himself undone the patriotic ties 44 *wants* lacks
46 *confirm* verify by imposing 48 *home* off 49 *by my troth* on my word

VOLUMNIA

50 Anger's my meat. I sup upon myself,
And so shall starve with feeding. Come, let's go.

52 Leave this faint puling, and lament as I do,
In anger, Juno-like. Come, come, come.

MENENIUS   Fie, fie, fie!

                                            Exeunt.

*

❧ **IV.3** *Enter a Roman and a Volsce.*

ROMAN   I know you well, sir, and you know me. Your
name, I think, is Adrian.

VOLSCE   It is so, sir. Truly, I have forgot you.

ROMAN   I am a Roman; and my services are, as you are,
against 'em. Know you me yet?

VOLSCE   Nicanor, no?

ROMAN   The same, sir.

VOLSCE   You had more beard when I last saw you, but
9   your favor is well appeared by your tongue. What's the
10   news in Rome? I have a note from the Volscian state
11   to find you out there. You have well saved me a day's
journey.

ROMAN   There hath been in Rome strange insurrections:
the people against the senators, patricians, and nobles.

VOLSCE   Hath been? Is it ended then? Our state thinks
not so. They are in a most warlike preparation, and
hope to come upon them in the heat of their division.

ROMAN   The main blaze of it is past, but a small thing
would make it flame again, for the nobles receive so to
20   heart the banishment of that worthy Coriolanus that
21   they are in a ripe aptness to take all power from the
people and to pluck from them their tribunes forever.

---

52 *puling* whimpering
IV.3 The highway to Antium   **9** *favor* face; *appeared* made apparent   **11**
find you out seek   **21** *in a ripe aptness* strongly inclined

This lies glowing, I can tell you, and is almost mature
for the violent breaking out.

VOLSCE Coriolanus banished?

ROMAN Banished, sir.

VOLSCE You will be welcome with this intelligence, 27
Nicanor.

ROMAN The day serves well for them now. I have heard 29
it said, the fittest time to corrupt a man's wife is when 30
she's fall'n out with her husband. Your noble Tullus Aufidius will appear well in these wars, his great opposer,
Coriolanus, being now in no request of his country.

VOLSCE He cannot choose. I am most fortunate, thus 34
accidentally to encounter you. You have ended my
business, and I will merrily accompany you home.

ROMAN I shall, between this and supper, tell you most 37
strange things from Rome, all tending to the good of
their adversaries. Have you an army ready, say you?

VOLSCE A most royal one: the centurions and their 40
charges, distinctly billeted, already in th' entertain- 41
ment, and to be on foot at an hour's warning.

ROMAN I am joyful to hear of their readiness and am the
man, I think, that shall set them in present action. So,
sir, heartily well met, and most glad of your company.

VOLSCE You take my part from me, sir. I have the most
cause to be glad of yours.

ROMAN Well, let us go together.   *Exeunt.*

*

---

27 *intelligence* news 29 *them* the Volscians 34 *choose* help appearing well
37 *this* now 40 *centurions* officers each commanding a century – i.e., a
hundred men 41 *distinctly* separately 41–42 *entertainment* service

  IV.4 *Enter Coriolanus in mean apparel, disguised and muffled.*

CORIOLANUS
  A goodly city is this Antium. City,
  'Tis I that made thy widows. Many an heir
3 Of these fair edifices fore my wars
  Have I heard groan and drop. Then know me not,
  Lest that thy wives with spits and boys with stones
6 In puny battle slay me.
     Enter a Citizen.   Save you, sir.
CITIZEN
  And you.
CORIOLANUS   Direct me, if it be your will,
8 Where great Aufidius lies. Is he in Antium?
CITIZEN
  He is, and feasts the nobles of the state
10 At his house this night.
CORIOLANUS   Which is his house, beseech you?
CITIZEN
  This, here before you.
CORIOLANUS   Thank you, sir. Farewell.
                              Exit Citizen.
  O world, thy slippery turns! Friends now fast sworn,
  Whose double bosoms seems to wear one heart,
  Whose hours, whose bed, whose meal and exercise
15 Are still together; who twin, as 'twere, in love
16 Unseparable, shall within this hour,
17 On a dissension of a doit, break out
18 To bitterest enmity. So, fellest foes,
  Whose passions and whose plots have broke their sleep
20 To take the one the other, by some chance,
21 Some trick not worth an egg, shall grow dear friends

IV.4 Before the house of Aufidius in Antium   **3** *edifices* buildings; *fore* before
6 *puny* petty; *Save* God save   **8** *lies* lodges   **15** *still* always   **16** *this* an   **17**
dissension . . . doit trivial dispute   **18** *fellest* fiercest   **21** *trick* trifle

And interjoin their issues. So with me.   22
My birthplace hate I, and my love 's upon
This enemy town. I'll enter. If he slay me,
He does fair justice; if he give me way,   25
I'll do his country service.   *Exit.*

*

⌇ **IV.5** *Music plays. Enter a Servingman.*

FIRST SERVINGMAN   Wine, wine, wine! What service is
   here? I think our fellows are asleep.   *[Exit.]* 2
      Enter another Servingman.
SECOND SERVINGMAN   Where's Cotus? My master calls
   for him. Cotus!   *Exit.*
      Enter Coriolanus.
CORIOLANUS
   A goodly house. The feast smells well, but I
   Appear not like a guest.
      Enter the first Servingman.
FIRST SERVINGMAN   What would you have, friend?
   Whence are you? Here's no place for you. Pray, go to
   the door.   *Exit.*
CORIOLANUS
   I have deserved no better entertainment,   10
   In being Coriolanus.
      Enter second Servant.
SECOND SERVINGMAN   Whence are you, sir? Has the
   porter his eyes in his head, that he gives entrance to
   such companions? Pray, get you out.   14
CORIOLANUS   Away!
SECOND SERVINGMAN   Away? get you away!
CORIOLANUS   Now th' art troublesome.
SECOND SERVINGMAN   Are you so brave? I'll have you   18
   talked with anon.   19

---

22 *interjoin their issues* join fortunes 25 *give me way* grant my request
   IV.5 Within the house of Aufidius 2 *fellows* companions 10 *entertain-*
ment reception 14 *companions* riffraff 18 *brave* insolent 19 *anon* at once

Enter third Servingman; the first meets him.

20 THIRD SERVINGMAN What fellow's this?

FIRST SERVINGMAN A strange one as ever I looked on. I cannot get him out o' th' house. Prithee, call my master to him.

THIRD SERVINGMAN What have you to do here, fellow?
25 Pray you, avoid the house.

CORIOLANUS Let me but stand; I will not hurt your hearth.

THIRD SERVINGMAN What are you?

CORIOLANUS A gentleman.

30 THIRD SERVINGMAN A marv'lous poor one.

CORIOLANUS True, so I am.

THIRD SERVINGMAN Pray you, poor gentleman, take up
33 some other station. Here's no place for you. Pray you, avoid. Come.

35 CORIOLANUS Follow your function, go, and batten on cold bits.

Pushes him away from him.

THIRD SERVINGMAN What, you will not? Prithee, tell my master what a strange guest he has here.

SECOND SERVINGMAN And I shall.

Exit second Servingman.

40 THIRD SERVINGMAN Where dwell'st thou?

41 CORIOLANUS Under the canopy.

THIRD SERVINGMAN Under the canopy?

CORIOLANUS Ay.

THIRD SERVINGMAN Where's that?

45 CORIOLANUS I' th' city of kites and crows.

THIRD SERVINGMAN I' th' city of kites and crows?
47 What an ass it is! Then thou dwell'st with daws too?

CORIOLANUS No, I serve not thy master.

THIRD SERVINGMAN How, sir? Do you meddle with my
50 master?

---

25 *avoid* leave 30 *marv'lous* curiously 33 *station* place 35 *Follow your function* attend to your tasks; *batten* grow fat 41 *canopy* sky (metaphorical) 45 *kites and crows* birds of prey 47 *daws* foolish birds

CORIOLANUS   Ay, 'tis an honester service than to meddle
with thy mistress. Thou prat'st, and prat'st. Serve with
thy trencher. Hence!   53
    Beats him away.
    Enter Aufidius with the [second] Servingman.
AUFIDIUS   Where is this fellow?
SECOND SERVINGMAN   Here, sir. I'd have beaten him like
a dog, but for disturbing the lords within.
AUFIDIUS
Whence com'st thou? What wouldst thou? Thy name?
Why speak'st not? Speak, man. What's thy name?
CORIOLANUS   If, Tullus,
Not yet thou know'st me, and, seeing me, dost not
Think me for the man I am, necessity   60
Commands me name myself.   61
AUFIDIUS   What is thy name?
CORIOLANUS
A name unmusical to the Volscians' ears,
And harsh in sound to thine.
AUFIDIUS   Say, what's thy name?
Thou hast a grim appearance, and thy face
Bears a command in't; though thy tackle 's torn,
Thou show'st a noble vessel. What's thy name?
CORIOLANUS
Prepare thy brow to frown. Know'st thou me yet?
AUFIDIUS
I know thee not. Thy name?
CORIOLANUS
My name is Caius Martius, who hath done
To thee particularly and to all the Volsces   70
Great hurt and mischief; thereto witness may
My surname, Coriolanus. The painful service,   72
The extreme dangers, and the drops of blood
Shed for my thankless country are requited

----

53 *trencher* plate; *Hence* get away **60** *Think* take **61** *name* to name **72**
painful laborious

75 But with that surname – a good memory,
And witness of the malice and displeasure
Which thou shouldst bear me. Only that name remains.
78 The cruelty and envy of the people,
79 Permitted by our dastard nobles, who
80 Have all forsook me, hath devoured the rest,
81 And suffered me by th' voice of slaves to be
82 Whooped out of Rome. Now this extremity
Hath brought me to thy hearth, not out of hope –
Mistake me not – to save my life; for if
I had feared death, of all the men i' th' world
86 I would have 'voided thee, but in mere spite,
87 To be full quit of those my banishers,
Stand I before thee here. Then if thou hast
89 A heart of wreak in thee, that wilt revenge
90 Thine own particular wrongs, and stop those maims
Of shame seen through thy country, speed thee straight,
And make my misery serve thy turn. So use it
That my revengeful services may prove
As benefits to thee; for I will fight
95 Against my cank'red country with the spleen
96 Of all the under fiends. But if so be
97 Thou dar'st not this, and that to prove more fortunes
Th' art tired, then, in a word, I also am
Longer to live most weary, and present
100 My throat to thee and to thy ancient malice;
Which not to cut would show thee but a fool,
Since I have ever followed thee with hate,
103 Drawn tuns of blood out of thy country's breast,
104 And cannot live but to thy shame unless
It be to do thee service.

AUFIDIUS   O Martius, Martius!
Each word thou hast spoke hath weeded from my heart

---

75 *memory* memorial   78 *cruelty and envy* envious cruelty   79 *dastard* cowardly   81 *suffered* allowed   82 *Whooped* shouted   86 *mere* pure   87 *full quit of* completely even with   89 *heart of wreak* vengeful heart   90 *maims* injuries   95 *cank'red* corrupted; *spleen* anger   96 *under* infernal   97 *prove* try   100 *ancient* longstanding   103 *tuns* barrels   104 *but to* except to

A root of ancient envy. If Jupiter
Should from yond cloud speak divine things,
And say "'Tis true," I'd not believe them more
Than thee, all-noble Martius. Let me twine   *110*
Mine arms about thy body, whereagainst   111
My grainèd ash an hundred times hath broke,   112
And scarred the moon with splinters. Here I clip   113
The anvil of my sword, and do contest
As hotly and as nobly with thy love
As ever in ambitious strength I did
Contend against thy valor. Know thou first,
I loved the maid I married; never man
Sighed truer breath. But that I see thee here,
Thou noble thing, more dances my rapt heart   120
Than when I first my wedded mistress saw
Bestride my threshold. Why, thou Mars, I tell thee,   122
We have a power on foot, and I had purpose   123
Once more to hew thy target from thy brawn,   124
Or lose mine arm for't. Thou hast beat me out   125
Twelve several times, and I have nightly since   126
Dreamt of encounters 'twixt thyself and me.
We have been down together in my sleep,   128
Unbuckling helms, fisting each other's throat,   129
And waked half dead with nothing. Worthy Martius,   130
Had we no other quarrel else to Rome, but that   131
Thou art thence banished, we would muster all
From twelve to seventy, and, pouring war
Into the bowels of ungrateful Rome,
Like a bold flood o'erbear't. O, come, go in,   135
And take our friendly senators by th' hands,
Who now are here, taking their leaves of me,
Who am prepared against your territories,

---

111 *whereagainst* against which   112 *grainèd ash* wooden lance   113 *clip*
embrace   120 *rapt* enraptured   122 *Bestride* step over   123 *power on foot*
army mobilized   124 *target* shield; *brawn* muscular arm   125 *out* thoroughly   126 *several* different   128 *been down* struggling on the ground
129 *helms* helmets   130 *waked* I have awakened   131 *to* against   135 *o'erbear't* overflow violently

Though not for Rome itself.

CORIOLANUS   You bless me, gods!

AUFIDIUS

140   Therefore, most absolute sir, if thou wilt have
     The leading of thine own revenges, take

142   Th' one half of my commission; and set down –
     As best thou art experienced, since thou know'st
     Thy country's strength and weakness – thine own ways,
     Whether to knock against the gates of Rome,
     Or rudely visit them in parts remote,

147   To fright them ere destroy. But come in.
     Let me commend thee first to those that shall
     Say yea to thy desires. A thousand welcomes!

150   And more a friend than e'er an enemy;
     Yet, Martius, that was much. Your hand. Most wel-
     come!   *Exeunt.*

         Enter two of the Servingmen.

FIRST SERVINGMAN   Here's a strange alteration!

SECOND SERVINGMAN   By my hand, I had thought to
154   have strucken him with a cudgel; and yet my mind gave
     me his clothes made a false report of him.

FIRST SERVINGMAN   What an arm he has! He turned me
     about with his finger and his thumb as one would set
     up a top.

SECOND SERVINGMAN   Nay, I knew by his face that there
160   was something in him. He had, sir, a kind of face,
     methought – I cannot tell how to term it.

FIRST SERVINGMAN   He had so, looking as it were –
     Would I were hanged, but I thought there was more in
     him than I could think.

SECOND SERVINGMAN   So did I, I'll be sworn. He is sim-
166   ply the rarest man i' th' world.

FIRST SERVINGMAN   I think he is. But a greater soldier
168   than he you wot on.

---

140 *absolute* perfect   142 *commission* command; *set down* decide   147 *ere destroy* before destroying them   154 *gave* suggested to   166 *rarest* most remarkable   168 *wot on* know of

SECOND SERVINGMAN Who, my master?

FIRST SERVINGMAN Nay, it's no matter for that.   170

SECOND SERVINGMAN Worth six on him.

FIRST SERVINGMAN Nay, not so neither. But I take him
to be the greater soldier.

SECOND SERVINGMAN Faith, look you, one cannot tell
how to say that. For the defense of a town, our general
is excellent.

FIRST SERVINGMAN Ay, and for an assault too.

Enter the third Servingman.

THIRD SERVINGMAN O slaves, I can tell you news. News,
you rascals!

BOTH [FIRST AND SECOND] What, what, what? Let's   180
partake.

THIRD SERVINGMAN I would not be a Roman, of all na-
tions. I had as lief be a condemned man.

BOTH Wherefore? Wherefore?

THIRD SERVINGMAN Why, here's he that was wont to
thwack our general, Caius Martius.

FIRST SERVINGMAN Why do you say "thwack our general"?

THIRD SERVINGMAN I do not say "thwack our general,"
but he was always good enough for him.   190

SECOND SERVINGMAN Come, we are fellows and friends.
He was ever too hard for him; I have heard him say so
himself.

FIRST SERVINGMAN He was too hard for him directly, to
say the troth on't. Before Corioles he scotched him and   195
notched him like a carbonado.   196

SECOND SERVINGMAN An he had been cannibally given,   197
he might have broiled and eaten him too.

FIRST SERVINGMAN But more of thy news?

THIRD SERVINGMAN Why, he is so made on here within,   200
as if he were son and heir to Mars; set at upper end o'

---

170 *it's . . . that* never mind about names **195** *troth* truth; *scotched* slashed
196 *carbonado* meat scored for broiling **197** *An* if; *given* inclined **200**
made on made much of

th' table; no question asked him by any of the senators,
203 but they stand bald before him. Our general himself
204 makes a mistress of him; sanctifies himself with's hand,
and turns up the white o' th' eye to his discourse. But
the bottom of the news is, our general is cut i' th' middle and but one half of what he was yesterday; for the
other has half, by the entreaty and grant of the whole
209 table. He'll go, he says, and sowl the porter of Rome
210 gates by th' ears. He will mow all down before him, and
211 leave his passage polled.

SECOND SERVINGMAN And he's as like to do't as any man
I can imagine.

THIRD SERVINGMAN Do't? he will do't! for, look you, sir,
he has as many friends as enemies; which friends, sir, as
it were, durst not, look you, sir, show themselves, as we
217 term it, his friends whilst he's in directitude.

FIRST SERVINGMAN Directitude? what's that?

THIRD SERVINGMAN But when they shall see, sir, his
220 crest up again, and the man in blood, they will out
221 of their burrows like conies after rain, and revel all with
him.

FIRST SERVINGMAN But when goes this forward?

224 THIRD SERVINGMAN Tomorrow, today, presently. You
shall have the drum struck up this afternoon. 'Tis, as it
226 were, a parcel of their feast, and to be executed ere they
wipe their lips.

SECOND SERVINGMAN Why, then we shall have a stirring
world again. This peace is nothing but to rust iron, in-
230 crease tailors, and breed ballad-makers.

FIRST SERVINGMAN Let me have war, say I. It exceeds
peace as far as day does night. It's sprightly, waking,
233 audible, and full of vent. Peace is a very apoplexy,

---

203 *but* unless; *bald* bareheaded **204** *sanctifies . . . hand* touches his hand
as if it were a sacred relic **209** *sowl* pull roughly **211** *polled* shorn **217** *directitude* discredit (verbal blunder) **220** *crest* comb (as in cockfighting); *in
blood* full of vitality **221** *conies* rabbits **224** *presently* immediately **226**
parcel part **233** *audible* capable of hearing; *vent* savor; *apoplexy* paralysis

lethargy; mulled, deaf, sleepy, insensible; a getter of 234
more bastard children than war's a destroyer of men.

SECOND SERVINGMAN   'Tis so, and as war, in some sort,
may be said to be a ravisher, so it cannot be denied but 237
peace is a great maker of cuckolds.   238

FIRST SERVINGMAN   Ay, and it makes men hate one another.   240

THIRD SERVINGMAN   Reason: because they then less need
one another. The wars for my money. I hope to see
Romans as cheap as Volscians. They are rising, they are
rising.

BOTH [FIRST AND SECOND]   In, in, in, in!   *Exeunt.*

*

∾ **IV.6** *Enter the two Tribunes, Sicinius and Brutus.*

SICINIUS
We hear not of him, neither need we fear him.
His remedies are tame: the present peace   2
And quietness of the people, which before
Were in wild hurry. Here do we make his friends
Blush that the world goes well, who rather had,   5
Though they themselves did suffer by't, behold
Dissentious numbers pest'ring streets than see   7
Our tradesmen singing in their shops and going
About their functions friendly.

BRUTUS
We stood to't in good time.   10
     Enter Menenius.   Is this Menenius?

SICINIUS
'Tis he, 'tis he! O, he is grown most kind of late. –
Hail, sir!

_____

234 *mulled* stupefied; *getter* begetter   238 *cuckolds* men whose wives are un-
faithful

IV.6 A public place in Rome   2 *His remedies* the remedies against him;
tame mild   5 *rather had* would rather have   7 *pest'ring* crowding   10 *stood
to't* took a stand

MENENIUS   Hail to you both!

SICINIUS   Your Coriolanus
Is not much missed, but with his friends.
The commonwealth doth stand, and so would do,
Were he more angry at it.

MENENIUS
All's well, and might have been much better if
18   He could have temporized.

SICINIUS   Where is he, hear you?

MENENIUS
Nay, I hear nothing. His mother and his wife
20   Hear nothing from him.

Enter three or four Citizens.

ALL
21   The gods preserve you both!

SICINIUS   Good-e'en, our neighbors.

BRUTUS
Good-e'en to you all, good-e'en to you all.

FIRST CITIZEN
Ourselves, our wives, and children, on our knees,
Are bound to pray for you both.

SICINIUS   Live, and thrive!

BRUTUS
Farewell, kind neighbors.
We wished Coriolanus had loved you as we did.

CITIZENS
Now the gods keep you!

BOTH TRIBUNES   Farewell, farewell.

Exeunt Citizens.

SICINIUS
28   This is a happier and more comely time
Than when these fellows ran about the streets,
30   Crying confusion.

BRUTUS   Caius Martius was
A worthy officer i' th' war, but insolent,

---

18 *temporized* compromised   21 *Good-e'en* good evening   28 *comely* decent

O'ercome with pride, ambitious past all thinking,
Self-loving –   33
SICINIUS   And affecting one sole throne
Without assistance.   34
MENENIUS   I think not so.
SICINIUS
We should by this, to all our lamentation,   35
If he had gone forth consul, found it so.
BRUTUS
The gods have well prevented it, and Rome
Sits safe and still without him.
     Enter an Aedile.
AEDILE   Worthy tribunes,
There is a slave whom we put in prison
Reports the Volsces with two several powers   40
Are entered in the Roman territories,
And with the deepest malice of the war
Destroy what lies before 'em.
MENENIUS   'Tis Aufidius,
Who, hearing of our Martius' banishment,
Thrusts forth his horns again into the world;
Which were inshelled when Martius stood for Rome,   46
And durst not once peep out.
SICINIUS
Come, what talk you of Martius?
BRUTUS
Go see this rumorer whipped. It cannot be
The Volsces dare break with us.   50
MENENIUS   Cannot be!
We have record that very well it can,
And three examples of the like hath been
Within my age. But reason with the fellow,   53
Before you punish him, where he heard this,
Lest you shall chance to whip your information   55

---

33 *affecting* desiring   34 *assistance* partners   35 *by this* by now   40 *several*
separate   46 *inshelled* drawn in; *stood* stood up   53 *reason with* question ra-
tionally   55 *information* source of information

And beat the messenger who bids beware
Of what is to be dreaded.

SICINIUS   Tell not me.
I know this cannot be.

BRUTUS   Not possible.

Enter a Messenger.

MESSENGER
The nobles in great earnestness are going
60 All to the Senate House. Some news is coming
61 That turns their countenances.

SICINIUS   'Tis this slave –
62 Go whip him 'fore the people's eyes – his raising,
Nothing but his report.

MESSENGER   Yes, worthy sir.
64 The slave's report is seconded, and more,
65 More fearful, is delivered.

SICINIUS   What more fearful?

MESSENGER
It is spoke freely out of many mouths –
How probable I do not know – that Martius,
Joined with Aufidius, leads a power 'gainst Rome,
69 And vows revenge as spacious as between
70 The young'st and oldest thing.

SICINIUS   This is most likely!

BRUTUS
71 Raised only, that the weaker sort may wish
72 Good Martius home again.

SICINIUS   The very trick on't.

MENENIUS
This is unlikely.
74 He and Aufidius can no more atone
75 Than violent'st contrariety.

Enter [another] Messenger.

---

61 *turns* changes 62 *raising* incitement 64 *seconded* confirmed 65 *delivered* reported 69–70 *as spacious . . . thing* embracing all 71 *Raised* set going 72 *on't* of it 74 *atone* be reconciled 75 *violent'st contrariety* opposite extremes

MESSENGER
You are sent for to the Senate.
A fearful army, led by Caius Martius
Associated with Aufidius, rages
Upon our territories, and have already
O'erborne their way, consumed with fire, and took 80
What lay before them.
    Enter Cominius.
COMINIUS   O, you have made good work!
MENENIUS
What news? What news?
COMINIUS
You have holp to ravish your own daughters and 83
To melt the city leads upon your pates, 84
To see your wives dishonored to your noses –
MENENIUS
What's the news? What's the news?
COMINIUS
Your temples burnèd in their cement, and
Your franchises, whereon you stood, confined 88
Into an auger's bore. 89
MENENIUS   Pray now, your news? –
You have made fair work, I fear me. – Pray, your news? – 90
If Martius should be joined with Volscians –
COMINIUS   If?
He is their god. He leads them like a thing
Made by some other deity than nature,
That shapes man better; and they follow him
Against us brats with no less confidence 95
Than boys pursuing summer butterflies
Or butchers killing flies.
MENENIUS   You have made good work,
You and your apron-men, you that stood so much

---

80 *O'erborne* overcome 83 *holp* helped 84 *leads* leaden roofs; *pates* heads
88 *franchises* political rights; *whereon you stood* on which you insisted 89
auger's bore smallest aperture 95 *brats* children

99	Upon the voice of occupation and
100	The breath of garlic-eaters!

COMINIUS   He'll shake
Your Rome about your ears.

MENENIUS   As Hercules
102   Did shake down mellow fruit. You have made fair work!

BRUTUS
But is this true, sir?

COMINIUS   Ay, and you'll look pale
Before you find it other. All the regions
105   Do smilingly revolt, and who resists
106   Are mocked for valiant ignorance,
107   And perish constant fools. Who is't can blame him?
Your enemies and his find something in him.

MENENIUS
We are all undone, unless
110   The noble man have mercy.

COMINIUS   Who shall ask it?
The tribunes cannot do't for shame; the people
Deserve such pity of him as the wolf
Does of the shepherds. For his best friends, if they
114   Should say "Be good to Rome," they charged him
            even
As those should do that had deserved his hate,
116   And therein showed like enemies.

MENENIUS   'Tis true.
If he were putting to my house the brand
118   That should consume it, I have not the face
119   To say, "Beseech you, cease." You have made fair
            hands,
120   You and your crafts! You have crafted fair!

---

99 *voice of occupation* mechanics' suffrage   102 *fruit* apples of Hesperides
105 *who* whoever   106 *valiant ignorance* foolish bravery   107 *constant* loyal
114 *charged* would enjoin   116 *showed* would appear   118 *face* brazenness
119 *made fair hands* done a fine job (ironic)   120 *crafted fair* intrigued
beautifully

COMINIUS   You have brought
  A trembling upon Rome, such as was never
  S' incapable of help.   122

TRIBUNES   Say not we brought it.

MENENIUS
  How? Was 't we? We loved him,
  But like beasts and cowardly nobles,
  Gave way unto your clusters, who did hoot   125
  Him out o' th' city.

COMINIUS   But I fear
  They'll roar him in again. Tullus Aufidius,
  The second name of men, obeys his points   128
  As if he were his officer. Desperation
  Is all the policy, strength, and defense   130
  That Rome can make against them.

    Enter a troop of Citizens.

MENENIUS   Here come the clusters.
  And is Aufidius with him? – You are they
  That made the air unwholesome, when you cast
  Your stinking greasy caps in hooting at
  Coriolanus' exile. Now he's coming;
  And not a hair upon a soldier's head
  Which will not prove a whip. As many coxcombs   137
  As you threw caps up will he tumble down,
  And pay you for your voices. 'Tis no matter.
  If he could burn us all into one coal,   140
  We have deserved it.

ALL CITIZENS
  Faith, we hear fearful news.   142

FIRST CITIZEN   For mine own part,
  When I said "Banish him," I said 'twas pity.

SECOND CITIZEN   And so did I.

THIRD CITIZEN   And so did I; and, to say the truth, so
  did very many of us. That we did, we did for the best;

---

122 *S' incapable of help* so beyond help   125 *clusters* crowds   128 *of* among;
points directions   137 *coxcombs* fool's caps   142 *For . . . part* speaking for
myself

and though we willingly consented to his banishment,
yet it was against our will.

COMINIUS
You're goodly things, you voices!

MENENIUS   You have made good work,
150   You and your cry! Shall's to the Capitol?

COMINIUS
O, ay, what else?   *Exeunt both.*

SICINIUS
Go, masters, get you home; be not dismayed.
153   These are a side that would be glad to have
This true, which they so seem to fear. Go home,
And show no sign of fear.

FIRST CITIZEN   The gods be good to us! Come, masters,
let's home. I ever said we were i' th' wrong when we
banished him.

SECOND CITIZEN   So did we all. But come, let's home.
                              Exeunt Citizens.

BRUTUS
160   I do not like this news.

SICINIUS   Nor I.

BRUTUS
161   Let's to the Capitol. Would half my wealth
Would buy this for a lie!

SICINIUS   Pray, let us go.
                              Exeunt Tribunes.

                    *

∿ IV.7 *Enter Aufidius, with his Lieutenant.*

AUFIDIUS
Do they still fly to th' Roman?

LIEUTENANT
I do not know what witchcraft's in him, but

---

150 *cry* pack; *Shall's* shall us   153 *side* faction   161–62 *Would . . . lie* I
would give half my fortune if this were untrue
    IV.7 A camp near Rome

Your soldiers use him as the grace 'fore meat,
Their talk at table, and their thanks at end;
And you are dark'ned in this action, sir,   5
Even by your own.
AUFIDIUS   I cannot help it now,
Unless by using means I lame the foot   7
Of our design. He bears himself more proudlier,
Even to my person, than I thought he would
When first I did embrace him. Yet his nature   10
In that's no changeling, and I must excuse   11
What cannot be amended.
LIEUTENANT   Yet I wish, sir –
I mean for your particular – you had not   13
Joined in commission with him, but either   14
Had borne the action of yourself, or else
To him had left it solely.
AUFIDIUS
I understand thee well; and be thou sure,
When he shall come to his account, he knows not   18
What I can urge against him. Although it seems,   19
And so he thinks, and is no less apparent   20
To th' vulgar eye, that he bears all things fairly,   21
And shows good husbandry for the Volscian state,   22
Fights dragonlike, and does achieve as soon   23
As draw his sword, yet he hath left undone
That which shall break his neck or hazard mine,   25
Whene'er we come to our account.
LIEUTENANT
Sir, I beseech you, think you he'll carry Rome?   27
AUFIDIUS
All places yield to him ere he sits down,   28
And the nobility of Rome are his;

---

5 *dark'ned* eclipsed   7 *means* means whereby   11 *In . . . changeling* is not in-
constant in that respect   13 *for your particular* in your own interests   14
commission command   18 *account* reckoning   19 *urge against* accuse him of
21 *vulgar* common   22 *husbandry* management   23 *achieve* carry out his
intention   25 *hazard* imperil   27 *carry* conquer   28 *ere . . . down* before he
lays siege

30 The senators and patricians love him too.
The tribunes are no soldiers, and their people
Will be as rash in the repeal as hasty
To expel him thence. I think he'll be to Rome
34 As is the osprey to the fish, who takes it
35 By sovereignty of nature. First he was
A noble servant to them, but he could not
37 Carry his honors even. Whether 'twas pride,
38 Which out of daily fortune ever taints
39 The happy man; whether defect of judgment,
40 To fail in the disposing of those chances
41 Which he was lord of; or whether nature,
42 Not to be other than one thing, not moving
43 From th' casque to th' cushion, but commanding peace
44 Even with the same austerity and garb
As he controlled the war; but one of these,
46 As he hath spices of them all – not all,
47 For I dare so far free him – made him feared,
So hated, and so banished. But he has a merit,
49 To choke it in the utt'rance. So our virtues
50 Lie in th' interpretation of the time,
And power, unto itself most commendable,
52 Hath not a tomb so evident as a chair
T' extol what it hath done.
One fire drives out one fire, one nail, one nail;
Rights by rights founder, strengths by strengths do fail.
Come, let's away. When, Caius, Rome is thine,
57 Thou art poor'st of all; then shortly art thou mine.

Exeunt.

*

---

34 *osprey* fish hawk   35 *sovereignty* predominance   37 *even* without losing his equilibrium   38 *daily fortune* uninterrupted success; *taints* corrupts   39 *happy* fortunate   40 *disposing* making good use of   41 *nature* character 42–43 *moving From* changing in the transition   43 *casque* general's helmet; *cushion* senator's seat   44 *garb* manner   46 *spices . . . all* a tincture of each 47 *free* absolve   49 *To . . . utt'rance* enough to suppress the recital of his faults   50 *the time* our contemporaries   52 *not . . . chair* no memorial so certain as a public rostrum   57 *shortly* soon

❧ **V.1** *Enter Menenius, Cominius; Sicinius, Brutus, the
two Tribunes; with others.*

MENENIUS
No, I'll not go. You hear what he hath said   1
Which was sometime his general, who loved him   2
In a most dear particular. He called me father.   3
But what o' that? Go, you that banished him;
A mile before his tent fall down, and knee   5
The way into his mercy. Nay, if he coyed   6
To hear Cominius speak, I'll keep at home.   7

COMINIUS
He would not seem to know me.   8

MENENIUS   Do you hear?

COMINIUS
Yet one time he did call me by my name.
I urged our old acquaintance, and the drops   10
That we have bled together. "Coriolanus"
He would not answer to, forbade all names.
He was a kind of nothing, titleless,
Till he had forged himself a name o' th' fire   14
Of burning Rome.

MENENIUS   Why, so! You have made good work!
A pair of tribunes that have racked for Rome,   16
To make coals cheap! A noble memory!   17

COMINIUS
I minded him how royal 'twas to pardon   18
When it was less expected. He replied
It was a bare petition of state   20
To one whom they had punished.

MENENIUS   Very well.
Could he say less?

V.1 A public place in Rome   2 *Which* who; *sometime* formerly   3 *In . . .
particular* with warmest personal affection   5 *knee* crawl   6 *coyed* disdained
7 *keep* stay   8 *would not seem* pretended not   14 *o'* out of   16 *racked* striven
17 *memory* memorial   18 *minded* reminded   20 *bare petition of state* mere
political plea

COMINIUS

23   I offered to awaken his regard
    For's private friends. His answer to me was
25   He could not stay to pick them in a pile
    Of noisome, musty chaff. He said 'twas folly,
    For one poor grain or two, to leave unburnt
28   And still to nose th' offense.

MENENIUS   For one poor grain or two?
    I am one of those! His mother, wife, his child,
30   And this brave fellow too, we are the grains.
    You are the musty chaff, and you are smelt
    Above the moon. We must be burnt for you.

SICINIUS
    Nay, pray, be patient. If you refuse your aid
34   In this so-never-needed help, yet do not
    Upbraid's with our distress. But, sure, if you
    Would be your country's pleader, your good tongue,
37   More than the instant army we can make,
    Might stop our countryman.

MENENIUS   No, I'll not meddle.

SICINIUS
    Pray you, go to him.

MENENIUS   What should I do?

BRUTUS
40   Only make trial what your love can do
    For Rome toward Martius.

MENENIUS   Well, and say that Martius
42   Return me, as Cominius is returned,
    Unheard – what then?
44   But as a discontented friend, grief-shot
    With his unkindness? Say't be so?

---

23 *offered* attempted   25 *stay . . . them* stop to pick them out   28 *nose* smell; *offense* offensive matter   34 *so-never-needed* never so much needed   37 *instant* hastily mustered   42 *Return* send away   44 *grief-shot* sorrow-stricken

SICINIUS   Yet your good will
  Must have that thanks from Rome, after the measure   46
  As you intended well.
MENENIUS   I'll undertake't:
  I think he'll hear me. Yet, to bite his lip
  And hum at good Cominius much unhearts me.   49
  He was not taken well; he had not dined.   50
  The veins unfilled, our blood is cold, and then
  We pout upon the morning, are unapt
  To give or to forgive; but when we have stuffed
  These pipes and these conveyances of our blood   54
  With wine and feeding, we have suppler souls   55
  Than in our priestlike fasts. Therefore I'll watch him   56
  Till he be dieted to my request,   57
  And then I'll set upon him.

BRUTUS
  You know the very road into his kindness,
  And cannot lose your way.   60
MENENIUS   Good faith, I'll prove him,
  Speed how it will. I shall ere long have knowledge
  Of my success.   *Exit.*   62
COMINIUS   He'll never hear him.
SICINIUS   Not?
COMINIUS
  I tell you, he does sit in gold, his eye   63
  Red as 'twould burn Rome, and his injury   64
  The jailer to his pity. I kneeled before him.
  'Twas very faintly he said, "Rise"; dismissed me
  Thus, with his speechless hand. What he would do
  He sent in writing after me; what he would not,
  Bound with an oath to yield to his conditions;   69

46–47 *after . . . As* to the extent that   49 *hum* (an inarticulate sound of displeasure); *unhearts* disheartens   50 *taken well* approached opportunely   54 *conveyances* channels   55 *suppler* more yielding   56 *watch* wait for   57 *dieted to* fed to the point of entertaining   60 *prove* try   62 *success* result   63 *does . . . gold* is enthroned   64 *injury* sense of injury   69 *Bound* he bound; *to yield* that we should yield

70   So that all hope is vain
71   Unless his noble mother and his wife,
      Who, as I hear, mean to solicit him
      For mercy to his country. Therefore let's hence,
74   And with our fair entreaties haste them on.   *Exeunt.*

✴

✷ **V.2** *Enter Menenius to the Watch on guard.*

FIRST WATCH
    Stay. Whence are you?
SECOND WATCH   Stand, and go back.
MENENIUS
    You guard like men; 'tis well. But, by your leave,
    I am an officer of state, and come
    To speak with Coriolanus.
FIRST WATCH   From whence?
MENENIUS   From Rome.
FIRST WATCH
    You may not pass; you must return. Our general
    Will no more hear from thence.
SECOND WATCH
    You'll see your Rome embraced with fire before
8   You'll speak with Coriolanus.
MENENIUS   Good my friends,
    If you have heard your general talk of Rome
10   And of his friends there, it is lots to blanks
    My name hath touched your ears. It is Menenius.
FIRST WATCH
12   Be't so; go back. The virtue of your name
13   Is not here passable.
MENENIUS   I tell thee, fellow,
14   Thy general is my lover. I have been

---

71 *Unless* except for 74 *fair* courteous
   V.2 The Volscian camp before Rome 8 *Good my friends* my good friends
10 *lots* prizes; *blanks* lottery tickets without value 12 *virtue* power 13 *passable* current 14 *lover* well-wisher

The book of his good acts, whence men have read
His fame unparalleled, haply amplified; 16
For I have ever verified my friends, 17
Of whom he's chief, with all the size that verity
Would without lapsing suffer. Nay, sometimes, 19
Like to a bowl upon a subtle ground, 20
I have tumbled past the throw; and in his praise 21
Have almost stamped the leasing. Therefore, fellow, 22
I must have leave to pass.

FIRST WATCH Faith, sir, if you had told as many lies in
his behalf as you have uttered words in your own, you
should not pass here; no, though it were as virtuous to
lie as to live chastely. Therefore go back. 27

MENENIUS Prithee, fellow, remember my name is Menenius, always factionary on the party of your general. 29

SECOND WATCH Howsoever you have been his liar, as 30
you say you have, I am one that, telling true under him,
must say you cannot pass. Therefore go back.

MENENIUS Has he dined, canst thou tell? For I would
not speak with him till after dinner.

FIRST WATCH You are a Roman, are you?

MENENIUS I am, as thy general is.

FIRST WATCH Then you should hate Rome, as he does.
Can you, when you have pushed out your gates the 38
very defender of them, and in a violent popular ignorance given your enemy your shield, think to front his 40
revenges with the easy groans of old women, the vir-
ginal palms of your daughters, or with the palsied inter- 42
cession of such a decayed dotant as you seem to be? 43
Can you think to blow out the intended fire your city is
ready to flame in with such weak breath as this? No,
you are deceived; therefore back to Rome, and prepare

---

16 *haply* possibly; *amplified* exaggerated 17 *verified* supported the credit of
19 *lapsing* falling into falsehood 20 *bowl* wooden ball; *subtle* deceptive 21
tumbled past the throw overshot 22 *stamped* attested; *leasing* falsehood 27
chastely honestly 29 *factionary* partisan 38 *out* out of 40 *front* appease
42–43 *intercession* pleading 43 *dotant* dotard

for your execution. You are condemned; our general
48   has sworn you out of reprieve and pardon.
MENENIUS   Sirrah, if thy captain knew I were here, he
50   would use me with estimation.
FIRST WATCH   Come, my captain knows you not.
MENENIUS   I mean thy general.
FIRST WATCH   My general cares not for you. Back, I say,
  go! lest I let forth your half pint of blood. Back! –
55   That's the utmost of your having. Back!
MENENIUS   Nay, but, fellow, fellow –
    Enter Coriolanus and Aufidius.
CORIOLANUS   Now what's the matter?
58 MENENIUS   Now, you companion, I'll say an errand for
  you. You shall know now that I am in estimation; you
60   shall perceive that a Jack guardant cannot office me
61   from my son Coriolanus. Guess but by my enter-
62   tainment with him if thou stand'st not i' th' state of
63   hanging, or of some death more long in spectatorship
  and crueler in suffering. Behold now presently, and
65   swound for what's to come upon thee. *[To Coriolanus]*
  The glorious gods sit in hourly synod about thy particular prosperity, and love thee no worse than thy old father
  Menenius does! O my son, my son! Thou art preparing
  fire for us. Look thee, here's water to quench it. I was
70   hardly moved to come to thee, but being assured none
  but myself could move thee, I have been blown out of
  our gates with sighs, and conjure thee to pardon Rome
73   and thy petitionary countrymen. The good gods assuage
74   thy wrath, and turn the dregs of it upon this varlet here –
75   this, who, like a block, hath denied my access to thee.
CORIOLANUS   Away!

---

48 *out of* beyond   50 *use* treat; *estimation* esteem   55 *the . . . having* as
much as you have   58 *companion* fellow (contemptuous)   60 *Jack guardant*
knave on guard; *office* officiously keep   61–62 *entertainment* reception
62–63 *if . . . hanging* if you are not in a condition to be hanged   63 *spectatorship* watching   65 *swound* faint   70 *hardly* with difficulty   73 *petitionary*
entreating   74 *varlet* rogue   75 *block* obstruction, blockhead

MENENIUS   How? away?

CORIOLANUS

Wife, mother, child, I know not. My affairs
Are servanted to others. Though I owe   79
My revenge properly, my remission lies   80
In Volscian breasts. That we have been familiar,
Ingrate forgetfulness shall poison rather   82
Than pity note how much. Therefore be gone.
Mine ears against your suits are stronger than
Your gates against my force. Yet, for I loved thee,   85
Take this along. I writ it for thy sake,
   [Gives a letter.]
And would have sent it. Another word, Menenius,
I will not hear thee speak. This man, Aufidius,
Was my beloved in Rome; yet thou behold'st!

AUFIDIUS

You keep a constant temper.   90
                Exeunt. Manent the Guard and Menenius.

FIRST WATCH   Now, sir, is your name Menenius?

SECOND WATCH   'Tis a spell, you see, of much power.
You know the way home again.

FIRST WATCH   Do you hear how we are shent for keeping 94
your greatness back?

SECOND WATCH   What cause do you think I have to
swound?

MENENIUS   I neither care for th' world nor your general.
For such things as you, I can scarce think there's any,
you're so slight. He that hath a will to die by himself 100
fears it not from another. Let your general do his worst.
For you, be that you are, long, and your misery increase 102
with your age! I say to you, as I was said to, "Away!"
                                                    Exit.

---

79 *servanted* made subservient; *owe* possess   80 *properly* as my own; *remission* power to pardon   82 *Ingrate forgetfulness* your ingratitude in failing to defend me   85 *for* because   94 *shent* taken to task   100 *by himself* at his own hands   102 *long* tedious, long-lived

FIRST WATCH   A noble fellow, I warrant him.

SECOND WATCH   The worthy fellow is our general. He's
the rock, the oak not to be wind-shaken.   *Exit Watch.*

*

∾ **V.3** *Enter Coriolanus and Aufidius [with others].*

CORIOLANUS
We will before the walls of Rome tomorrow

2   Set down our host. My partner in this action,

3   You must report to th' Volscian lords how plainly

4   I have borne this business.

AUFIDIUS   Only their ends
You have respected; stopped your ears against
The general suit of Rome; never admitted
A private whisper, no, not with such friends
That thought them sure of you.

CORIOLANUS   This last old man,
Whom with a cracked heart I have sent to Rome,

10 Loved me above the measure of a father;

11 Nay, godded me indeed. Their latest refuge
Was to send him; for whose old love I have –

13 Though I showed sourly to him – once more offered
The first conditions, which they did refuse

15 And cannot now accept. To grace him only,
That thought he could do more, a very little

17 I have yielded to. Fresh embassies and suits,
Nor from the state nor private friends, hereafter
Will I lend ear to.
    Shout within.   Ha! What shout is this?

20 Shall I be tempted to infringe my vow
In the same time 'tis made? I will not.

V.3 Before the tent of Coriolanus **2** *host* army **3** *plainly* straightforwardly
4 *borne* conducted **11** *godded* idolized; *latest* last **13** *showed* acted **15**
grace gratify **17–18** *Fresh . . . friends* neither fresh embassies from the state
nor suits from private friends

Enter Virgilia, Volumnia, Valeria, young Martius,
with Attendants.

My wife comes foremost; then the honored mold   22
Wherein this trunk was framed, and in her hand   23
The grandchild to her blood. But out, affection!   24
All bond and privilege of nature, break!
Let it be virtuous to be obstinate.
What is that curt'sy worth, or those doves' eyes,
Which can make gods forsworn? I melt, and am not   28
Of stronger earth than others. My mother bows,
As if Olympus to a molehill should   30
In supplication nod; and my young boy   31
Hath an aspect of intercession which   32
Great nature cries, "Deny not!" Let the Volsces
Plow Rome and harrow Italy! I'll never
Be such a gosling to obey instinct, but stand   35
As if a man were author of himself
And knew no other kin.

VIRGILIA   My lord and husband!

CORIOLANUS
These eyes are not the same I wore in Rome.

VIRGILIA
The sorrow that delivers us thus changed   39
Makes you think so.   40

CORIOLANUS   Like a dull actor now,
I have forgot my part, and I am out,   41
Even to a full disgrace. Best of my flesh,
Forgive my tyranny, but do not say
For that "Forgive our Romans." O, a kiss
Long as my exile, sweet as my revenge!
Now, by the jealous queen of heaven, that kiss   46
I carried from thee dear, and my true lip   47

---

22 *mold* matrix 23 *trunk* body 24 *out, affection* away with partiality 28
forsworn breakers of their word 30 *Olympus* sacred mountain 31 *supplication* pleading 32 *aspect* look 35 *gosling* baby goose 39 *delivers* shows 41
out at fault 46 *queen of heaven* Juno 47 *dear* cherished

48   Hath virgined it e'er since. You gods! I prate,
    And the most noble mother of the world
50   Leave unsaluted. Sink, my knee, i' th' earth;
      Kneels.
    Of thy deep duty more impression show
    Than that of common sons.

VOLUMNIA   O, stand up blest!
    Whilst with no softer cushion than the flint
    I kneel before thee, and unproperly
    Show duty as mistaken all this while
    Between the child and parent.

CORIOLANUS   What is this?
57   Your knees to me? To your corrected son?
58   Then let the pebbles on the hungry beach
59   Fillip the stars! Then let the mutinous winds
60   Strike the proud cedars 'gainst the fiery sun,
61   Murd'ring impossibility to make
    What cannot be, slight work.

VOLUMNIA   Thou art my warrior;
63   I holp to frame thee. Do you know this lady?

CORIOLANUS
64   The noble sister of Publicola,
    The moon of Rome, chaste as the icicle
66   That's curded by the frost from purest snow
67   And hangs on Dian's temple – dear Valeria!

VOLUMNIA
68   This is a poor epitome of yours,
69   Which by th' interpretation of full time
70   May show like all yourself.

CORIOLANUS   The god of soldiers,
    With the consent of supreme Jove, inform
    Thy thoughts with nobleness, that thou mayst prove

---

48 *virgined it* kept it unviolated 57 *corrected* chastised 58 *hungry* barren
59 *Fillip* snap with a finger 61 *Murd'ring impossibility* making nothing
seem impossible 63 *holp* helped 64 *Publicola* a famous consul 66 *curded*
congealed 67 *Dian* virgin goddess 68 *epitome* miniature 69 *interpretation* elaboration (oratorical) 70 *show* appear

To shame unvulnerable, and stick i' th' wars　　　　73
Like a great sea mark, standing every flaw　　　　74
And saving those that eye thee!　　　　75

VOLUMNIA　　　　　　　　Your knee, sirrah.

CORIOLANUS
That's my brave boy!

VOLUMNIA
Even he, your wife, this lady, and myself,
Are suitors to you.

CORIOLANUS　　　　I beseech you, peace!
Or, if you'd ask, remember this before:
The thing I have forsworn to grant may never　　　　80
Be held by you denials. Do not bid me　　　　81
Dismiss my soldiers, or capitulate　　　　82
Again with Rome's mechanics. Tell me not
Wherein I seem unnatural. Desire not
T' allay my rages and revenges with
Your colder reasons.

VOLUMNIA　　　　　　　O, no more, no more!
You have said you will not grant us anything,
For we have nothing else to ask but that
Which you deny already; yet we will ask,
That, if you fail in our request, the blame　　　　90
May hang upon your hardness. Therefore hear us.

CORIOLANUS
Aufidius, and you Volsces, mark; for we'll
Hear naught from Rome in private. – Your request?

VOLUMNIA
Should we be silent and not speak, our raiment
And state of bodies would bewray what life　　　　95
We have led since thy exile. Think with thyself
How more unfortunate than all living women

---

73 *To shame unvulnerable* incapable of disgrace; *stick* be fixed　74 *sea mark*
point serving as guide for navigators; *flaw* gust　75 *sirrah* sir　80 *forsworn*
sworn not　81 *denials* personal refusals　82 *capitulate* come to terms　90
fail in fail to grant　95 *bewray* betray

Are we come hither, since that thy sight, which should
Make our eyes flow with joy, hearts dance with comforts,
100 Constrains them weep and shake with fear and sorrow,
Making the mother, wife, and child to see
The son, the husband, and the father tearing
103 His country's bowels out. And to poor we
104 Thine enmity 's most capital. Thou barr'st us
Our prayers to the gods, which is a comfort
That all but we enjoy. For how can we,
Alas, how can we for our country pray,
Whereto we are bound, together with thy victory,
109 Whereto we are bound? Alack, or we must lose
110 The country, our dear nurse, or else thy person,
Our comfort in the country. We must find
112 An evident calamity, though we had
Our wish which side should win. For either thou
114 Must as a foreign recreant be led
With manacles through our streets, or else
Triumphantly tread on thy country's ruin,
117 And bear the palm for having bravely shed
Thy wife and children's blood. For myself, son,
I purpose not to wait on fortune till
120 These wars determine. If I cannot persuade thee
121 Rather to show a noble grace to both parts
Than seek the end of one, thou shalt no sooner
March to assault thy country than to tread –
Trust to't, thou shalt not – on thy mother's womb
That brought thee to this world.

VIRGILIA   Ay, and mine,
That brought you forth this boy, to keep your name
127 Living to time.

BOY   A shall not tread on me!
I'll run away till I am bigger, but then I'll fight.

---

100 *weep* to weep   103 *poor we* our poor selves   104 *capital* deadly; *barr'st us* keep us from   109 *or* either   112 *evident* certain   114 *recreant* traitor
117 *palm* emblem of triumph   120 *determine* end   121 *grace* mercy; *parts* sides   127 *A* he (familiar)

CORIOLANUS
  Not of a woman's tenderness to be
  Requires nor child nor woman's face to see.   *130*
  I have sat too long.
    [Rises.]
VOLUMNIA   Nay, go not from us thus.
  If it were so that our request did tend
  To save the Romans, thereby to destroy
  The Volsces whom you serve, you might condemn us
  As poisonous of your honor. No, our suit
  Is that you reconcile them while the Volsces
  May say "This mercy we have showed," the Romans,
  "This we received," and each in either side
  Give the all-hail to thee and cry, "Be blest   139
  For making up this peace!" Thou know'st, great son,   *140*
  The end of war's uncertain, but this certain,
  That, if thou conquer Rome, the benefit
  Which thou shalt thereby reap is such a name
  Whose repetition will be dogged with curses,
  Whose chronicle thus writ: "The man was noble,   145
  But with his last attempt he wiped it out,   146
  Destroyed his country, and his name remains
  To th' ensuing age abhorred." Speak to me, son.
  Thou hast affected the fine strains of honor,   149
  To imitate the graces of the gods;   *150*
  To tear with thunder the wide cheeks o' th' air,
  And yet to change thy sulphur with a bolt   152
  That should but rive an oak. Why dost not speak?   153
  Think'st thou it honorable for a noble man
  Still to remember wrongs? Daughter, speak you.
  He cares not for your weeping. Speak thou, boy.
  Perhaps thy childishness will move him more
  Than can our reasons. There's no man in the world
  More bound to's mother, yet here he lets me prate

---

139 *all-hail* salutation of honor   145 *chronicle* history; *writ* will be written
146 *it* his nobility   149 *affected* desired; *fine strains* refinements   152 *sulphur* lightning; *with* for; *bolt* thunderbolt   153 *rive* split

160   Like one i' th' stocks. Thou hast never in thy life
161   Showed thy dear mother any courtesy,
162   When she, poor hen, fond of no second brood,
       Has clucked thee to the wars, and safely home
       Loaden with honor. Say my request 's unjust,
       And spurn me back; but if it be not so,
166   Thou art not honest, and the gods will plague thee
167   That thou restrain'st from me the duty which
       To a mother's part belongs. *He turns away.*
       Down, ladies! Let us shame him with our knees.
170   To his surname Coriolanus 'longs more pride
       Than pity to our prayers. Down! An end!
       This is the last. So, we will home to Rome,
173   And die among our neighbors. Nay, behold's!
       This boy, that cannot tell what he would have
       But kneels and holds up hands for fellowship,
176   Does reason our petition with more strength
       Than thou hast to deny't. Come, let us go.
178   This fellow had a Volscian to his mother;
       His wife is in Corioles, and this child
180   Like him by chance. Yet give us our dispatch.
       I am hushed until our city be afire,
182   And then I'll speak a little.
       [Coriolanus] holds her by the hand, silent.
   CORIOLANUS   O mother, mother!
183   What have you done? Behold, the heavens do ope,
       The gods look down, and this unnatural scene
       They laugh at. O my mother, mother! O!
       You have won a happy victory to Rome;
       But for your son — believe it, O believe it! —
       Most dangerously you have with him prevailed,
189   If not most mortal to him. But let it come.
190   Aufidius, though I cannot make true wars,

---

160 *i' th' stocks* publicly humiliated   161 *courtesy* special consideration   162 *When* while; *fond* desirous   166 *honest* just   167 *That* because   170 *'longs* belongs   173 *behold's* behold us   176 *reason* argue for   178 *to* for   180 *dispatch* dismissal   182 *a little* i.e., a dying curse   183 *ope* open   189 *mortal* fatally

I'll frame convenient peace. Now, good Aufidius,   191
Were you in my stead, would you have heard   192
A mother less? Or granted less, Aufidius?

AUFIDIUS
I was moved withal.   194

CORIOLANUS   I dare be sworn you were!
And, sir, it is no little thing to make
Mine eyes to sweat compassion. But, good sir,
What peace you'll make, advise me. For my part,
I'll not to Rome, I'll back with you; and pray you,
Stand to me in this cause. O mother! wife!   199

AUFIDIUS *[Aside]*
I am glad thou hast set thy mercy and thy honor   200
At difference in thee. Out of that I'll work
Myself a former fortune.   202

CORIOLANUS *[To Volumnia]* Ay, by and by.
But we will drink together; and you shall bear
A better witness back than words, which we,   204
On like conditions, will have counter-sealed.
Come, enter with us. Ladies, you deserve
To have a temple built you. All the swords
In Italy, and her confederate arms,   208
Could not have made this peace.   *Exeunt.*

*

❧ **V.4** *Enter Menenius and Sicinius.*

MENENIUS   See you yond coign o' th' Capitol, yond cor-   1
nerstone?
SICINIUS   Why, what of that?
MENENIUS   If it be possible for you to displace it with
your little finger, there is some hope the ladies of Rome,
especially his mother, may prevail with him. But I say

---

191 *convenient* appropriate   192 *stead* place   194 *withal* i.e., by it   199
Stand to support   202 *former fortune* fortune like my former one   204
which i.e., the treaty   208 *confederate arms* military allies
   V.4 A street in Rome   1 *coign* corner

7   there is no hope in't; our throats are sentenced and stay
     upon execution.

SICINIUS   Is't possible that so short a time can alter the
10   condition of a man?

11 MENENIUS   There is difference between a grub and a
     butterfly; yet your butterfly was a grub. This Martius is
     grown from man to dragon. He has wings; he's more
     than a creeping thing.

SICINIUS   He loved his mother dearly.

MENENIUS   So did he me, and he no more remembers his
     mother now than an eight-year-old horse. The tartness
     of his face sours ripe grapes. When he walks, he moves
19   like an engine, and the ground shrinks before his tread-
20   ing. He is able to pierce a corslet with his eyes, talks like
21   a knell and his hum is a battery. He sits in his state, as a
22   thing made for Alexander. What he bids be done is
23   finished with his bidding. He wants nothing of a god
     but eternity, and a heaven to throne in.

SICINIUS   Yes, mercy, if you report him truly.

26 MENENIUS   I paint him in the character. Mark what
     mercy his mother shall bring from him. There is no
     more mercy in him than there is milk in a male tiger.
29   That shall our poor city find; and all this is long of you.

30 SICINIUS   The gods be good unto us!

MENENIUS   No, in such a case the gods will not be good
     unto us. When we banished him, we respected not
     them, and, he returning to break our necks, they re-
     spect not us.

     Enter a Messenger.

MESSENGER
     Sir, if you'd save your life, fly to your house.
     The plebeians have got your fellow tribune,
37   And hale him up and down, all swearing, if

7–8 *stay upon* wait for   11 *differency* difference   19 *engine* instrument of
war   20 *corslet* body armor   21 *battery* assault; *state* throne   22 *thing . . .
Alexander* statue of Alexander the Great   23 *finished . . . bidding* accom-
plished as soon as ordered; *wants* lacks   26 *in the character* according to his
personality   29 *long of* owing to   37 *hale* pull

The Roman ladies bring not comfort home,
They'll give him death by inches.
    Enter another Messenger.
SICINIUS   What's the news?
MESSENGER
    Good news, good news! The ladies have prevailed,   40
    The Volscians are dislodged, and Martius gone.   41
    A merrier day did never yet greet Rome,
    No, not th' expulsion of the Tarquins.   43
SICINIUS   Friend,
    Art thou certain this is true? Is't most certain?
MESSENGER
    As certain as I know the sun is fire.
    Where have you lurked that you make doubt of it?   46
    Ne'er through an arch so hurried the blown tide   47
    As the recomforted through th' gates. Why, hark you!   48
        Trumpets, hautboys; drums beat; all together.
    The trumpets, sackbuts, psalteries, and fifes,   49
    Tabors and cymbals and the shouting Romans   50
    Make the sun dance. Hark you!
        A shout within.
MENENIUS   This is good news.
    I will go meet the ladies. This Volumnia
    Is worth of consuls, senators, patricians,
    A city full; of tribunes, such as you,
    A sea and land full. You have prayed well today.
    This morning for ten thousand of your throats
    I'd not have given a doit. Hark, how they joy!   57
        Sound still, with the shouts.
SICINIUS
    First, the gods bless you for your tidings; next,
    Accept my thankfulness.

---

41 *dislodged* retired   43 *Tarquins* dynasty of tyrants   46 *lurked* been hiding
47 *blown* swollen   48 *recomforted* reassured; **s.d.** *hautboys* oboes   49 *sackbuts* trombones; *psalteries* stringed instruments; *fifes* wind instruments   50
Tabors small drums   57 *doit* smallest possible sum

MESSENGER   Sir, we have all
60   Great cause to give great thanks.
SICINIUS   They are near the city?
MESSENGER
61   Almost at point to enter.
SICINIUS   We will meet them,
     And help the joy.   *Exeunt.*

*

❧ V.5   *Enter two Senators with Ladies [Volumnia, Vir-
        gilia, Valeria] passing over the stage, with other Lords.*

SENATOR
     Behold our patroness, the life of Rome!
     Call all your tribes together, praise the gods,
     And make triumphant fires; strew flowers before them.
     Unshout the noise that banished Martius;
5   Repeal him with the welcome of his mother.
     Cry "Welcome, ladies, welcome!"
ALL   Welcome, ladies,
     Welcome!
        A flourish with drums and trumpets. [Exeunt.]

*

❧ V.6   *Enter Tullus Aufidius, with Attendants.*

AUFIDIUS
     Go tell the lords o' th' city I am here.
2   Deliver them this paper. Having read it,
3   Bid them repair to th' marketplace, where I,
4   Even in theirs and in the commons' ears,
5   Will vouch the truth of it. Him I accuse
6   The city ports by this hath entered and

---

61 *at . . . enter* on the point of entering
    V.5 5 *Repeal him* recall him from exile
    V.6 A public place in Corioles   **2** *them* to them   **3** *repair* come   **4** *theirs*
their ears   **5** *Him* he whom   **6** *ports* gates

Intendst t' appear before the people, hoping
To purge himself with words. Dispatch.   8

> *[Exeunt Attendants.]*
> *Enter three or four Conspirators of Aufidius' faction.*

                                                    Most welcome!

FIRST CONSPIRATOR
How is it with our general?

AUFIDIUS   Even so
As with a man by his own alms empoisoned   *10*
And with his charity slain.

SECOND CONSPIRATOR   Most noble sir,
If you do hold the same intent wherein
You wished us parties, we'll deliver you   *13*
Of your great danger.

AUFIDIUS   Sir, I cannot tell.
We must proceed as we do find the people.

THIRD CONSPIRATOR
The people will remain uncertain whilst
'Twixt you there's difference; but the fall of either
Makes the survivor heir of all.

AUFIDIUS   I know it,
And my pretext to strike at him admits
A good construction. I raised him, and I pawned   20
Mine honor for his truth; who being so heightened,   21
He watered his new plants with dews of flattery,
Seducing so my friends; and to this end
He bowed his nature, never known before
But to be rough, unswayable, and free.   25

THIRD CONSPIRATOR
Sir, his stoutness   26
When he did stand for consul, which he lost
By lack of stooping –

AUFIDIUS   That I would have spoke of.
Being banished for't, he came unto my hearth;

---

8 *Dispatch* hurry 13 *parties* to be allies; *deliver* release 20 *construction* interpretation 21 *truth* loyalty; *heightened* exalted 25 *unswayable* unper-
suadable 26 *stoutness* obstinacy

30   Presented to my knife his throat. I took him,
31   Made him joint servant with me; gave him way
      In all his own desires; nay, let him choose
33   Out of my files, his projects to accomplish,
34   My best and freshest men; served his designments
35   In mine own person; holp to reap the fame
36   Which he did end all his; and took some pride
      To do myself this wrong; till at the last
      I seemed his follower, not partner, and
39   He waged me with his countenance as if
40   I had been mercenary.
FIRST CONSPIRATOR   So he did, my lord.
41   The army marveled at it; and in the last,
      When he had carried Rome and that we looked
43   For no less spoil than glory –
AUFIDIUS   There was it!
44   For which my sinews shall be stretched upon him.
45   At a few drops of women's rheum, which are
      As cheap as lies, he sold the blood and labor
      Of our great action; therefore shall he die,
48   And I'll renew me in his fall. But, hark!
        Drums and trumpets sound, with great shouts of the
        People.
FIRST CONSPIRATOR
49   Your native town you entered like a post,
50   And had no welcomes home; but he returns
      Splitting the air with noise.
SECOND CONSPIRATOR   And patient fools,
      Whose children he hath slain, their base throats tear
53   With giving him glory.
THIRD CONSPIRATOR   Therefore, at your vantage,
      Ere he express himself or move the people

---

31 *joint servant* colleague; *gave him way* gave way to him   33 *files* ranks   34
designments enterprises   35 *holp* helped   36 *end* gather in as a harvest   39
waged remunerated; *countenance* patronage   41 *marveled* was amazed   43
There that   44 *sinews . . . upon* strength shall be exerted against   45 *rheum*
tears   48 *renew me* be restored   49 *post* messenger   53 *at your vantage* seiz-
ing your opportunity

With what he would say, let him feel your sword,
Which we will second. When he lies along,   56
After your way his tale pronounced shall bury   57
His reasons with his body.
AUFIDIUS   Say no more.
Here come the lords.
   Enter the Lords of the city.
ALL LORDS
You are most welcome home.   60
AUFIDIUS   I have not deserved it.
But, worthy lords, have you with heed perused
What I have written to you?
ALL   We have.
FIRST LORD   And grieve to hear't.
What faults he made before the last, I think   63
Might have found easy fines; but there to end   64
Where he was to begin, and give away
The benefit of our levies, answering us   66
With our own charge, making a treaty where   67
There was a yielding – this admits no excuse.
AUFIDIUS
He approaches. You shall hear him.
   Enter Coriolanus, marching with Drum and Colors,
   the Commoners being with him.
CORIOLANUS
Hail, lords! I am returned your soldier;   70
No more infected with my country's love
Than when I parted hence, but still subsisting
Under your great command. You are to know
That prosperously I have attempted, and   74
With bloody passage led your wars even to   75
The gates of Rome. Our spoils we have brought home   76
Do more than counterpoise a full third part   77

---

56 *along* prone   **57** *your . . . pronounced* your own version of the affair   **58** *reasons* justifications   **62**   **63** *made* committed   **64** *fines* punishments   **66** *levies* forces raised; *answering* repaying   **67** *charge* expenses   **74** *prosperously . . . attempted* my endeavors have been fortunate   **75** *passage* course   **76** *spoils* plunder   **77** *Do . . . counterpoise* outweigh

The charges of the action. We have made peace
With no less honor to the Antiates
80 Than shame to th' Romans; and we here deliver,
81 Subscribed by th' consuls and patricians,
Together with the seal o' th' Senate, what
83 We have compounded on.

AUFIDIUS   Read it not, noble lords,
But tell the traitor in the highest degree
He hath abused your powers.

CORIOLANUS
Traitor? how now?

AUFIDIUS   Ay, traitor, Martius!

CORIOLANUS   Martius?

AUFIDIUS
Ay, Martius, Caius Martius! Dost thou think
I'll grace thee with that robbery, thy stol'n name
"Coriolanus" in Corioles?
90 You lords and heads o' th' state, perfidiously
He has betrayed your business and given up,
For certain drops of salt, your city Rome –
I say "your city" – to his wife and mother,
Breaking his oath and resolution like
95 A twist of rotten silk; never admitting
Counsel o' th' war; but at his nurse's tears
He whined and roared away your victory,
98 That pages blushed at him and men of heart
Looked wond'ring each at other.

CORIOLANUS   Hear'st thou, Mars?

AUFIDIUS
100 Name not the god, thou boy of tears!

CORIOLANUS   Ha!

AUFIDIUS   No more.

CORIOLANUS
Measureless liar, thou hast made my heart

---

81 *Subscribed* signed 83 *compounded* reached an agreement 90 *perfidiously* treacherously 95 *admitting* accepting 98 *That* so that; *heart* courage

Too great for what contains it. Boy? O slave!   102
Pardon me, lords, 'tis the first time that ever
I was forced to scold. Your judgments, my grave lords,
Must give this cur the lie; and his own notion –   105
Who wears my stripes impressed upon him, that   106
Must bear my beating to his grave – shall join
To thrust the lie unto him.

FIRST LORD
    Peace, both, and hear me speak.

CORIOLANUS
    Cut me to pieces, Volsces. Men and lads,   *110*
    Stain all your edges on me. Boy? False hound!   111
    If you have writ your annals true, 'tis there   112
    That, like an eagle in a dovecote, I
    Fluttered your Volscians in Corioles.
    Alone I did it. Boy?

AUFIDIUS   Why, noble lords,
    Will you be put in mind of his blind fortune,   116
    Which was your shame, by this unholy braggart,
    'Fore your own eyes and ears?

ALL CONSPIRATORS   Let him die for't.

ALL PEOPLE   Tear him to pieces! – Do it presently! –   119
    He killed my son! – My daughter! – He killed my   *120*
    cousin Marcus! He killed my father!

SECOND LORD
    Peace, ho! No outrage. Peace!
    The man is noble and his fame folds in   123
    This orb o' th' earth. His last offenses to us   124
    Shall have judicious hearing. Stand, Aufidius,   125
    And trouble not the peace.

CORIOLANUS   O that I had him,
    With six Aufidiuses, or more, his tribe,
    To use my lawful sword!

---

102 *Too . . . it* too swollen for my breast   **105** *notion* understanding   **106**
stripes impressed lashes imprinted   **111** *edges* swords   **112** *there* recorded
there   **116** *blind fortune* mere luck   **119** *presently* at once   **123** *folds in* en-
folds   **124** *orb* globe   **125** *judicious* judicial; *Stand* stop

AUFIDIUS   Insolent villain!
ALL CONSPIRATORS
   Kill, kill, kill, kill, kill him!
      Draw the Conspirators, and kill Martius, who falls.
      Aufidius stands on him.
LORDS   Hold, hold, hold, hold!
AUFIDIUS
130   My noble masters, hear me speak.
FIRST LORD   O Tullus –
SECOND LORD
   Thou hast done a deed whereat valor will weep.
THIRD LORD
   Tread not upon him. Masters all, be quiet!
133   Put up your swords.
AUFIDIUS
   My lords, when you shall know – as in this rage
   Provoked by him you cannot – the great danger
136   Which this man's life did owe you, you'll rejoice
137   That he is thus cut off. Please it your honors
138   To call me to your Senate. I'll deliver
   Myself your loyal servant, or endure
140   Your heaviest censure.
FIRST LORD   Bear from hence his body,
   And mourn you for him. Let him be regarded
142   As the most noble corse that ever herald
   Did follow to his urn.
SECOND LORD   His own impatience
   Takes from Aufidius a great part of blame.
   Let's make the best of it.
AUFIDIUS   My rage is gone,
146   And I am struck with sorrow. Take him up.
   Help, three o' th' chiefest soldiers; I'll be one.

---

133 *put up* sheathe   136 *did owe you* possessed for you   137 *Please it* may it
please   138 *deliver* show myself   142 *corse* corpse   146 *struck* afflicted

Beat thou the drum, that it speak mournfully.
Trail your steel pikes. Though in this city he
Hath widowed and unchilded many a one,   150
Which to this hour bewail the injury,
Yet he shall have a noble memory.   152
Assist.   *Exeunt, bearing the body of Coriolanus.*
                              A dead march sounded.

---

150 *unchilded* deprived of children   152 *memory* memorial